WORLD MISSIONS:
TOTAL SPIRITUAL WARFARE

World Missions: Total Spiritual Warfare

L. E. Maxwell

Kingsley Press

Shoals, Indiana

World Missions: Total Spiritual Warfare

PUBLISHED BY KINGSLEY PRESS
PO Box 973
Shoals, IN 47581
USA

Tel. (800) 971-7985
www.kingsleypress.com
E-mail: sales@kingsleypress.com

ISBN: 978-1-937428-35-8

Printed in the United States of America

Contents

Dedication

To the hundreds of "disciplined soldiers" at home and abroad who realize that there is "no discharge in (this) war" (Eccles. 8:8 ASV), these sermons are affectionately dedicated.

Publisher's Foreword

The book you hold in your hands is mostly unchanged from the original, which was first published in 1977. The title has been changed from *World Missions: Total War* to *World Missions: Total Spiritual Warfare* at the request of the copyright holders. Spelling has been regularized to American English. Additionally, the first chapter of the book has been modified very slightly by Paul Maxwell, the author's son.

We would like to express our sincere thanks to the copyright holders for permission to reprint this important work, and to Veronica Lewis in particular for her helpfulness as we worked through some of the details necessary to bring it to print.

May the Lord use the republishing of this classic work on world missions to stir up God's children everywhere with renewed zeal and purpose in the work of winning souls for King Jesus both abroad and on the home front.

Edward Cook
Kingsley Press
August 2013

L. E. Maxwell (1895-1984)

Preface

Missionary zeal is slacking off in many of our evangelical churches. It might be expected that missionary interest would be minimal among the liberals as a natural consequence of their false theology. But when fundamental folk fail to fulfil the Great Commission, we must needs ferret out the cause thereof. Such a blight does not just happen any more than the curse causeless does not come. In the Scriptures must be found the cause and the cure.

The whole Bible, read aright, is a missionary book. Bible teaching, expounded aright, begets missionary going and missionary giving. The gospel message, proclaimed aright, produces missionary outreach "among all nations."

All true Christians agree around the absolute necessity of Christ's dying and rising again as fundamental to their salvation. The risen Lord made plain to the whole group of assembled disciples the main theme of the Messianic Scriptures when he said: "Thus it is written, and thus it behoved Christ to suffer, and to rise from the dead the third day: and that repentance and remission of sins should be preached in his name among all nations" (Luke 24:46-47).

Thousands of pages have been penned by our theologians to fortify and further the great fundamentals of Christ's redemptive work. Other thousands have been written to promote particular Christian doctrines, to prove the plenary inspiration of Scripture, to preserve precious church ordinances—things which are good in themselves, all very good as far as they go.

But we must read on. The Lord of the harvest did not stop with the "thus-it-is-written" of his "dying and rising." He went on to point out the ultimate purpose of his glorious redemption: "And that repentance and remission of sins should be preached in his name among all nations" (v. 47).

Even as Christ was involved in the terrible necessity—"thus it is written, and thus it behoved Christ" to suffer and to rise again (v. 46), not less is coupled the inseparable and terrible necessity charged upon us: "*And that* repentance and remission of sins should be preached in his name among all nations" (v. 47). These twin necessities God has joined together. Let not man put them asunder.

However, as we search theological works, we can find volumes on verse 46 regarding the atoning work of Christ, but seldom can we discover so much as a paragraph on verse 47, which declares the ultimate purpose of Christ's redemptive work, viz. that the glad tidings should be "preached in his name among all nations." Manifestly the Great Commission (of verse 47) is the one great omission of most theologians. Yet here is the one great universal command to the church to preach the gospel to every creature; and he who is wise above that command is wise at his own risk and peril. The present missionary blight which has befallen us is the direct result of our downright disobedience to the ultimate purpose of our grand redemption.

We can thank God for the much missionary literature that has been forthcoming during the past decade. Yet there is a crying need for more Bible exposition on missions. Only thus can vision be re-established, and "where there is no vision the people perish." Oh, fellow-ministers and missionaries and church elders and Sunday school teachers, hearken! Let our teaching and preaching be crammed with Scripture expositions setting forth God's ultimate purpose to reach the regions beyond. Then, having laid well those foundations in a fresh "opening of our understanding to understand the Scriptures," let those expositions be supplemented and illustrated with fresh facts and figures from foreign fields.

"Facts are the fingers of God. To know the facts of modern missions is the necessary condition of intelligent interest. Knowledge does not always kindle zeal, but zeal is according to knowledge, and will not exist without it. A fire may be fanned with wind, but it must be fed with fuel; and facts are the fuel of this sacred flame, to be gathered, then scattered as burning brands to be as live coals elsewhere" (A. T. Pierson).

These sermons are sent forth with the hope that God's servants everywhere may come to revived missionary activity through a fresh insight into "Missions" as the main theme taught in the Scriptures. That these messages may prove to be fuel to fire the reader's faith and zeal is the prayer of the author.

Bugle Call to Christian Soldiers!
Shall your brethren go to war,
and shall ye sit here? (Numbers 32:6)

Your brethren—shall they go to war,
    And bear the toil and pain,
While idly you remain at home,
    Engrossed in selfish gain?
Perish the thought! Let all respond,
    And war with might and main.

Our brethren have gone out to fight
    Against unnumbered foes:
They wrestle not with flesh and blood,
    But Satan's hosts oppose;
Equipped with weapons from our God,
    They heed not wounds or woes.

Our brethren have the price once paid,
    No discharge now they want;
But shall they go alone to war,
    Forgotten at the front?
Have we no sense of shame that they
    Alone should bear the brunt?

Is there no part that you can play
    In this unceasing fight,
While all around you soldiers die
    With never help in sight?
Each one can intercede that they
    Will triumph in God's might.

"Be sure your sin will find you out"—
    This warning let us heed;
And now begin with earnest heart
    To meet our brother's need;
And let our help be not in word,
    But by our every deed.

May he who is our captain strong
    Stir all our hearts anew,
Until we rally round
    His cross united with the few.
Then in the midst of battle fierce
    The crown will come to view.

—T. S. Rendall

1

World Missions—Total War

D r. Stuart Holden declared a great Bible fact when he said: "The gospel contains, not only a promise of bliss, but a proclamation of battle." We have been flooded with the gospel's "promise of bliss," but have little literature on the "proclamation of battle."

The Lord Jesus declared that his advent would issue in strife, discord, and conflict: "Think not that I am come to send peace on earth: I came not to send peace, but a sword" (Matt. 10:34). He says in substance: "Disciples of mine, make no mistake, entertain no false conceptions. Peace is offered *through* me, but strife and conflict will be caused *by* me. Two humanities will be in conflict, centering around my acceptance or my rejection. While my real intent is to plant, propagate, and promote peace, the issue and event of my coming (on account of the lust and corruption of mankind) can only mean *war—spiritual warfare*."

Enlisted

The Christian's calling is a summons, a call to arms. Paul's epistles bristle with battle terms. We are called not to a holiday, but to a campaign. Our tent is pitched not in a paradise, but on the field of battle. We may view Christian missions as a job, a task, a service, a program, an assignment, an investment, a supreme effort. In a sense, perhaps, all of these aspects are true. But when Paul summoned Timothy "into the force," he charged him: "Endure hardship, as a good soldier of Christ Jesus" (2 Tim. 2:3 WEB). The primary and only adequate figure of Christian service is that of the military conflict. Timothy must first regard missionary service as a campaign, a battle, a conquest—war. Fight he must, and so fight "that he may please him who enlisted him as a soldier" (2 Tim. 2:4 NKJV).

World missions under Christ's captaincy means war, total war, total mobilization for total conflict—"armed with unshakeable resolve." And such a total warfare "means total commitment with no option and no returns, and past the point of no return" (Francis Steele). We are enlisted for life. Ours is the day of battle, and remember, O Christian soldier, "there is no discharge in the time of war" (Eccles. 8:8 NASB).

With the death of General Douglas MacArthur, the United States lost one of its great generals. Writing about his background, *Newsweek* aptly said that MacArthur was "born to battle." Of every born-again believer it may be said that he, too, has been "born to battle," spiritual conflict.

Eternal Conflict

We must keep our sights clear regarding the never-ending conflict between the kingdom of light and the kingdom of darkness, with

> Truth forever on the scaffold,
> Wrong forever on the throne.

Consider that when Christ was on their hands all the warring princes of this world, "Herod and Pontius Pilate, with the Gentiles and the people of Israel, were gathered together ... against the Lord, and against his Christ" (Acts 4:26-27). Satan is not divided against himself. These elements, though separated racially, politically, and religiously by astronomical dimensions, all fell into one another's arms—"gathered together"—in one united cry, "Crucify him, crucify him."

And this vile world has not abated one iota in its relentless hostility to Christ. Until this hour there abides an undying antagonism between righteousness and unrighteousness, a natural antagonism between light and darkness. A great gulf is forever fixed between heaven and hell. There remains, therefore, an essential hostility between Christ and Satan. That war is still on.

It is not surprising, then, that Christ likens the world to a battlefield. Under the figure of soldiery and warfare Christ says to his disciples: "He that is not with me is against me" (Luke 11:23). So dreadful are these battling antagonisms, so dreadful the issues, that "in my ranks," cries our captain, "there can be no rivals. My soldiers must be all for me, or they are against me. I can tolerate no divided allegiance, no reserve, no compromise, no halfheartedness. All attempted neutrality, even when well meant, is treason."

The Front Is Everywhere

Some sixty years ago the Edinburgh Conference of Missions adopted as its noble motto: "Crown Jesus Christ King." Muslim students, meeting simultaneously in Cairo, flung this warring reaction back into the teeth of the Christians: "Islam defies your Jesus."

This is one example of the fact that we are confronted with the world's outright declaration of total war—on Christ. We must confess that good soldiery is the lost chord of today's western Christianity.

Oh yes, we believe in being dedicated, committed, consecrated—to a lovely Jesus, to a beautiful, well-behaved life—but to war? Never! We are men of peace—at any price. And what a price! "The children of Ephraim, being armed, and carrying bows"—fully armed—"turned back in the day of battle" (Psa. 78:9). How like them we are! Never had we a better trained, a better equipped number of Christian young people—and never less willingness to engage Satan, the enemy. Ours is an anaemic faith. Ours is that fatal inertia on the eve of battle—the crucial moment when most wars are lost.

Cry from the Front

One of the hardest things a front-line soldier ever has to endure, whether in the military world or in the missionary world, are the unknowing, unfeeling, unresponsive folk at home. Let me give you a page from a missionary's experience. He left his station and went exploring in a new needy area in the Far East. He said,

> I spent some days finding out roads and details, sleeping in dirty log houses, people about as wild as they could be, stark-naked men and women ... running from me for fear.... What were my reactions to this trip? Sadness, impatience, bordering on disgust.

Here's a vast new mission field, ready to be entered, waiting for many years because we have no missionaries to place there. Rich America, with its thousands of young people trained and ready for service, yet not one for these tribal areas. Over the radio, on my return to my station, I heard music from America, young people singing, "We've a story to tell to the nations"; but it all seemed a mockery. I switched it off.

What more can we do to get these people evangelized? Do the people take us seriously, or are we just miserable enthusiasts? We write books, make movies, send thousands of newsletters, spend our furloughs pleading for help, trying to get some to go as missionaries, and the people go out into eternity without Christ, while the church at home glibly sings missionary hymns.

We bewail the lack of men, soldierly men to meet the cries from the front-line soldiers. But we can only blame ourselves. We have gone soft—soft in giving, soft in living, soft in message. We have become so soft that we cannot produce real *men*. Young women are not quite so stubborn as men. That is the reason they go more readily. Until we have recovered masculinity in our living, in our ministry, and in our message, men will struggle to surrender to Christ's lordship. The missionary goes out to the foreign field, a soldier of the cross. He gets men to man his national churches. The missionary is himself a soldier. He begets soldiers.

Prod from the Past

An old warrior-writer says:

> The Christians who conquered the Roman Empire for Christ had the appearance of invaders from another world, who absolutely refused to be naturalized to this world. Their conduct filled their neighbors with the strangest perplexity; they were so careless of life, so careful of conscience, so willing to shed their own blood, so confident of the overcoming power of the blood of the Lamb, so unsubdued to the custom of the country in which they sojourned, so mindful of "that country [heaven] from which they came out."
>
> The help of the world, the favor of its rulers, the loan of its resources, the use of its methods they utterly refused, lest by employing these they might compromise their King. An "invading army" maintained from

an invisible base, and placing more confidence in the leadership of an unseen Commander [Christ] than in all the government help that might be offered—that was what so bewildered and angered the nationals, who often desired to make friends with the Christians without abandoning their own gods. But there can be no reasonable doubt that that age in which the church was so completely separated from the world was the age in which Christianity was the most victorious in the world.

Theodore Roosevelt called Anthony Wayne, Brigadier General at 34, "the greatest field general America ever produced." Wayne was better known as "Mad Anthony."

With the British encamped at Germantown, George Washington held one of his inevitable councils of war. Wayne was all for attacking without delay, but most of the other officers sat around the table offering innumerable excuses for holding back.

When all the dissenting votes were in, Washington turned to Wayne, sitting quietly in a corner, reading a book. "What would you say, General?"

Wayne slammed the book shut, then rose slowly to his feet, glaring defiance at the group of distinguished officers, "I'd say nothing, Sir. I'd fight" (*American Mercury*).

Suppose we quit our "inevitable councils" and "innumerable excuses" and begin to "glare defiance" at a Christianity that merely maintains drills, talks war, and plays church. Rise up, O men of God! Gird your armor on. Arm yourself with Christ and his Word (1 John 3:8b; John 12:31); with the Holy Spirit (Zechariah 4:6); with the Sword of the Spirit—the Word of God (Ephesians 5:17); with prevailing prayer (Ephesians 5:18); with a fearless testimony (Revelation 12:11); and with faith and a good conscience (1 Timothy 1:19).

As a soldier of Christ press the battle. Remain steadfast. Become skilled in using the weapons of our warfare, remembering they "are not carnal but mighty through God to the pulling down of [Satan's] strongholds" (2 Corinthians 10:4).

Ours is war—total war. Christ won this war and defeated the enemy at the cross. Ours is to appropriate and apply his victory. Then with the apostle Paul we can confidently declare, "Thanks be to God, who always leads us in triumph in Christ" (2 Corinthians 2:14 NASB).

Money

Dug from the mountain side
Or washed in the glen,
Servant am I or master of men.
Earn me, I bless you;
Steal me, I curse you;
Grasp me and hold me,
A fiend shall possess you.
Lie for me, die for me,
Covet me, take me—
Angel or devil,
I'm just what you make me.

—Author Unknown

(See Appendix A regarding The Right Use of Money.)

2

Making Eternal Friends

General Booth, founder of the Salvation Army, used to be taunted about his use of "tainted money." His good-natured reply (we are told) was, "There is only one taint about it—'taint enough."

What do men mean when they talk about tainted money? Actually there is no such thing. Money is neither moral nor immoral; it is amoral. There is neither good nor evil in money. It is not money that is the root of all evil. God's warning is: "The *love* of money is a root of all kinds of evil" (1 Tim. 6:10 ASV).

It is therefore the use of money that makes it good or evil. By means of money we either blast men or bless men. Bad men abuse others by the foul manner of filching them of their money. This is what leads men to speak of tainted money.

In the parable of the unjust steward (Luke 16:1–15) Christ sets forth the proper use of money, "the mammon of unrighteousness." In this parable, the "unrighteous mammon" is plainly God's money which man in his unrighteousness misappropriates as his own. He covets it, worships it, and serves it as his idol-master.

Jesus must often have been offended by man's reckless language regarding earthly property. He heard men boast of my goods, my lands, my barns, my house, my fortune, my soul, etc. Luke therefore concludes this parable by telling us that when the Pharisees, "who were lovers of money, heard all these things they scoffed at him" (Luke 16:14 ASV). Their master-passion was money, and the reign of such a passion, Jesus said, "is abomination in the sight of God" (v. 15). But let us look at:

The Parable Itself

"And he said also unto the disciples, There was a certain rich man, who had a steward; and the same was accused unto him that he was wasting his goods" (16:1 ASV). This "certain rich man" would likely be a landlord or an owner of a considerable estate—living perhaps in a distant city. He had engaged this "steward" to handle his business and to manage all his financial affairs.

Then the report reached the master that the steward had been "wasting his goods." Of course the certain rich man must represent God himself, Christ's disciples the mere tenants or stewards of God. It was D. L. Moody who once said: "Life is simply a stewardship, and not an ownership; a trust and not a gift. With a gift you may do as you please, but with a trust you must give an account."

Upon hearing the report regarding the unjust steward, the landlord decided that his manager could be "no longer steward" (v. 2). Yet his master allowed the fellow a handful of days in which to take inventory and turn over the business to some successor. This sudden summons came to the steward about the way the call of death will come to each one of us as Christ's disciples: "Set thine house in order: for thou shalt die, and not live" (Isa. 38:1). "Give an account of thy stewardship; for thou mayest be no longer steward" (Luke 16:2).

All at once the situation of this man becomes critical. He is doomed ere long to be jobless, houseless, homeless. His days are numbered. "When I am put out of my stewardship"—then what? "I am resolved what to do" (v. 4). To himself he says, "I must redeem the time, must make my remaining few days count. Are my master's goods still in my hands? So they are, and under my authority. I am resolved to use them in such a way as to get advantage from them when I shall have them no more. I must make sure of a refuge for the time when I shall be homeless."

Fortunate is the man who can take seriously the summons of death and can be so startled as to say, "I am resolved what to do." As disciples we still have our divine Master's goods in our hands. Death will soon wrench these goods from us, or rather wrench us from the goods. It will indeed be wisdom for us to handle these goods to eternal advantage during the brief days while we have them at our disposal. In this parable we have Christ's mind for the Christian businessman, the disciple's wise and far-sighted investment.

For this steward, time is fast running out. He will soon be without house or home. But he knows business people under him who have both houses and rooms to spare. He says to himself: "Let me then make these people my friends, that when I am turned out on the street, more than one house shall be open to receive me" (Godet). He immediately calls his lord's debtors to him and "quickly" makes some complete settlements.

He says to the first, "How much owest thou unto my lord?"

The debtor replies, "A hundred measures of oil."

He answers, "Sit down and write out a check for fifty, and I'll write over your account, 'Paid in full.' I have the right to do it. My master's business is in my hands."

"What a good deal!" reckons the debtor. With abounding gratitude he settles, assuring the steward: "You have made me your lifelong friend."

Thus the steward deals with each of his master's debtors. By his shrewd generosity he makes many friends and feathers his own nest for the future.

Strange generosity this! For if all we have belongs to God, then what we share with others is out of his property and his purse. It is only out of our master's goods ("that which is another's," v. 12) that we are so generous. Is this "a sort of holy unfaithfulness"?

The Parable Applied

Note how "the lord commended the unjust steward," this "steward of unrighteousness (v. 8 ASV marg.). For what did his master commend him? Certainly not for his injustice, but "because he had done wisely." His master had to recognize the shrewdness, the cleverness of this steward. And behold how his cleverness paid off. He has been "sacked," so to speak. Dejected and forlorn he goes down the street. He is jobless and homeless, but far from friendless.

Presently he meets that first debtor, who got a paid-in-full settlement for fifty cents on the dollar. That "lifelong friend" listens to the steward's tale: "I've lost my stewardship; I'm without a home, poor and destitute and friendless."

"Friendless?" says the debtor. "Nay, come with me. I can't forget you. When you had charge of your master's goods, you made me your friend. I have room enough and to spare. Come along and share my house and hospitality."

Thus the steward is taken into one home after another through the many friends he made before losing his stewardship.

Our Master sets forth the chief point of this parable in verse 9: "And I say unto you, Make to yourselves friends by means of the mammon of unrighteousness; that, when it shall fail, they may receive you into the eternal tabernacles" (ASV).

Jesus is saying to you and to me: Disciples of mine, be wise. As "sons of light" learn a lesson from the "sons of this age." Are they clever and shrewd for their world, the only world they know? You be as alert to your "own generation." Yours is "the world to come." Imitate in the right way the wisdom of "the unrighteous steward." Beware of hoarding the mammon of unrighteousness. Don't squander it or merely enjoy it; no, nor build big barns, nor fine houses.

Instead of building a bank account or spending on yourselves—a procedure that will profit you nothing hereafter when you will be in turn as poor and destitute as the dismissed steward—hasten to make for yourselves, with the goods of another (God's, v. 12) a host of personal friends who will be forever bound to you by ties of undying gratitude. Then after your removal from this present scene, "they"— the friends you have made, the souls won through your missionary giving and who passed on before you into the heavenly mansions— "may receive you into the eternal tabernacles."

A friend of mine had been a missionary in Japan for many years. When he finally returned to America, there was at the gangplank of the Western port a typical citizen stationed there just to welcome Americans home from distant shores. As that warm-hearted person met him with a great friendly hand and a welcome to the home-bound missionary, he said: "Come in, my friend, this country is all yours." How illustrative, he often said, of "that day" when he would step on heaven's shore and be welcomed there by converted heathen, souls who had gone on before, "friends" with the welcome: "Come in, my friend; this is your own country—all yours."

The writer's daughter, a missionary to the Japanese, was called upon by a poor unwed mother. That fallen girl had just killed her baby and was on her way to "end it all" by committing suicide. (The one recourse to redeem yourself from disgrace in that land is to take your life.) But this hopeless little woman had heard that the foreign missionary had some kind of hope. Before her last leap into the unending dark, she would go and inquire. And my daughter had the "joy unspeakable" of leading her to the Savior, "saving a soul from death and hiding a multitude of sins." That redeemed little lassie may already have crossed over to the other shore. She will be there waiting and watching, not merely for my daughter, but for a farmer from southern Alberta, who (by supporting my daughter) made himself her "eternal friend" by means of "the mammon of unrighteousness."

What can be more wonderful than to anticipate the greetings in the great beyond by a host of friends, all born anew and blood-washed, actual people who would not have been there at all had it not been that you and I "did wisely"—made these people our personal friends by using the "mammon of unrighteousness" to send them the saving gospel? Let the reader ask himself the question:

> Will anyone then at the beautiful gate
> Be waiting and watching for me?

Then hasten to make "friends," many friends.[1] Your stewardship is brief. Use your money, use the gifts still in your hands, use all you have for the supreme business of making eternal friendships. If you "wisely" use the mammon of unrighteousness, yours will be the joy to swell the song:

> Friends will be there I have (made) long ago;
> Joy like a river around me will flow.

Your stewardship is over. But there they stand! Friends forever! Friends you made long before! Friends to meet you and to greet you and to welcome you into the "eternal tabernacles."

---

1. See Appendix B.

The Missionary Call

My soul is not at rest. There comes a strange
And secret whisper in my spirit, like
A dream of night, that tells me I am on
Enchanted ground. Why live I here?
The vows of God are on me, and I may not stop
To play with shadows, or pluck earthly flowers,
Till I my work have done and rendered up
Account. The voice of my departed Lord:
"Go teach all nations," from the Eastern world
Comes on the night breeze and awakens my ear.

And I will go. I may no longer doubt
To give my friends, and house, and idol hopes,
And every tender tie that binds my heart
To thee, my country: Why should I regard
Earth's little store of borrowed sweets? I sure
Have had enough of bitter in my cup
To show that never was it His design
Who placed me here that I should live in ease
Or drink at pleasure's fountain. Henceforth, then,
It matters not if storm or sunshine be
My earthly lot, bitter or sweet my cup;
I only pray, "God fit me for the work—
God make me holy, and my spirit nerve
For the stern hour of strife." Let me but know
There is an arm unseen that holds me up,
An eye that kindly watches all my path,
Till I my weary pilgrimage have done;
Let me but know I have a Friend that waits
To welcome me to glory, and I joy
To tread the dark and death-fraught wilderness.

And when I come to stretch me for the last,
In unattended agony beneath
The cocoa's shade, or lift my dying eyes
From Afric's burning sand, it will be sweet
That I have toiled for other worlds than this.
I know I shall feel happier than to die
On softer bed. And if I should reach Heaven—
If one that hath so deeply, darkly sinned—
If one whom ruin and revolt have held
With such a fearful grasp—if one for whom
Satan hath struggled as he hath for me—
Should ever reach that blessed shore, oh, how
This heart will glow with gratitude and love!
And through the ages of eternal years,
Thus saved, my spirit never shall repent
That toil and suffering once were mine below.

—Rev. Nathan Brown, D.D.

3

Which World?

Train up a child in the way he should go (Proverbs 22:6).

W e pose a most relevant and solemn question for Christian parents and pastors: "For which world are we training our children?" We quote the Scripture: "Train up a child in the way he should go: and when he is old, he will not depart from it." Scripture relates the child to an existence that is commenced for eternity. Solomon makes it clear that our training will determine his temporal as well as his eternal destiny.

That training—training by a true master is far more than *teaching*—is to be so ordered and consistent, so based on the principles of Scripture as to ensure God's fulfilment of his promise of the child's eternal well-being.

We could present many practical considerations of Proverbs 22:6. Just here, however, we are concerned with the relation of our text to God's great missionary program. "Train up a child in the way he should go." Why are not more of our children going forth as missionaries? Wherein lies the fault? Do we want them to get ahead in this world, or do we want them to get going for God? Too often our Christian young people are trained for this present world, instead of for the captain of their salvation. If only we were "training up" our youngsters in *"the* way *they should go,"* many more of them would be *going*—going "into all the world," going to "the regions beyond," going to preach good tidings "where Christ has not been named."

Yet here is a Christian parent who reacts: "We can't expect all our children to be missionaries." How true! Not all Christian young people should go abroad. Some should hold the ropes, while others descend into the depths of heathen darkness. But we fear this instance of parental reaction was an excuse for past parental delinquency. Should not every Christian, whether at home or abroad, be God's missionary just where he is? "Each Christian a missionary"—such is "the way he should go."

Parents often offer some threadbare excuses. Here is but one: "Doesn't our own world need doctors and nurses and teachers?" Quite so! And our world gets them, plenty of them; in fact, far too great a proportion of them. Do we argue that some must "tarry by the stuff"(1 Sam. 30:24)? Let us be fair. The number of those who "go down to the battle" abroad cannot be compared with those who tarry by the stuff at home. Compare the number of doctors and nurses in our Western world with those in the untouched "regions beyond." The per capita comparison should put every self-excusing Christian to shame. Of course the still greater shame to be heaped on our Western churches and training institutions is the fact that the bulk of men and money is used on local and often overlapping efforts.

Too many young people from Christian homes are being trained, not to be disciplined soldiers for Christ, but to fulfil professional positions, to secure good jobs, to qualify as teachers, to be competent businessmen—in other words, trained with ability to make a good living in this world and to enjoy a measure of ease and comfort. To put the question squarely: For which world are our children being trained?

The subtle temptation faces parents about the time junior is coming up to his last year of high school. How will he be directed? What road will he take? The low road, or the high road? The low road to worldly ambition, or the high road of "My Utmost for His Highest"? It is at such a crisis time that many Christian parents fail to magnify the missionary calling to their children as the most desirable way to spend their one and only life.

Few fathers urge their sons to toss worldly rewards to the winds, to cut out creature comforts, and to obey Christ's last command to "Go preach." And few mothers covet for their dear daughters lives of service and sacrifice for Christ. Parents, rather, want their youngsters to go to college, to marry well, to make money, to enhance the family name, and to avoid undergoing the hardships they themselves endured when they were young people.

To our shame it must be said of us as parents that, though Christians, "we have become basically worldly in our outlook, and we are raising a generation of young folk who will give their finest talents to a corporation but not to Christ. We train them to do for money what they will not do for the master" (MacDonald). We teach them how to do that which is contradictory to all Christian discipleship, how to make the best of both worlds—*how to have all this and heaven besides.*

I am thinking of Jenny Lind. She was one of the greatest singers who charmed the world and adorned the profession of the Christian faith. She was known as the Swedish Nightingale. At the peak of her singing powers she suddenly quit opera to return to it nevermore.

Jenny Lind was once asked by a young lady, as she sat on the beach at Ostend, Belgium, with her Bible on her lap and her gaze fixed on the sun as it was setting in all its majestic glory over the gentle waves: "What made you leave the opera, Madame?"

She had stepped down at the very time of her coronation as queen of the opera world. Laying her hand upon her Bible, Jenny Lind replied: "Because, my dear, every day I was thinking less and less of *this* (pointing to her Bible), and (pointing to the glorious sunset)nothing of *that*, and so I gave it up without regret for a greater life." She was somewhat like Moses of old who exchanged a cross for a crown.

Coming down to this modern day, we are reminded of Jim Elliott, noble martyr among the Auca Indians, who said, "He is no fool who gives to the Lord that which he cannot keep, to gain that which he cannot lose."

How worthy was the great Apostle's ambition: "I aspired to preach the gospel not where Christ was already named" (Rom. 15:20, NASB). Concerning Paul's ambition, it has been well said: "This is the highest, deepest, widest, most Christlike emotion that ever filled a human breast" (Newell).

We believe it was that great preacher, Charles H. Spurgeon, who charged his own son: "If God calls you to be a missionary, don't shrivel up to be a king."

And it was William Carey, that worthy father of modern missions, who asked prayer for his son, Felix, who had accompanied him to India: "Pray for Felix, for he has accepted an ambassadorship with the British government." To William Carey, his son was shrivelling up to be the king's representative.

William MacDonald, whom we have already quoted, writes well on this subject. He says:

> One young believer I know went off to a well-known university to the great satisfaction of his relatives and friends. But God had dealings with him there, and he decided he was not getting the type of training he needed. The next time he came home he told his Christian father he wanted to drop out and serve the Lord.
>
> The dad realized that such a step might scuttle all his well-laid plans for his son's success. For several hours he presented his strong reasons why it would be unwise for the lad to do this. In the back of his mind, the father also anticipated the social stigma that would be attached to such a move.
>
> Finally the son looked his father squarely in the eye and asked, "Well, Dad, do you want me to go on for the Lord, or don't you?" Fortunately this proved to be the end of all opposition.[1]

Not all young men are as fortunate to have such a father. I am thinking of Robert A. Jaffray, a Toronto boy, the son of the editor of that great paper, the *Toronto Globe and Mail*. As a young Christian of twenty years Robert came under the influence of Dr. A. B. Simpson, who had founded the training school in New York city for the preparing of missionaries for his fast-growing missionary society.

Robert did not long ponder God's plan for his life. He decided to go to New York for training as his first step to the mission field. But what had such a fanatical (?) notion to do with the father's plan for his son? There is an oft-told story (apocryphal, says A. W. Tozer) that the elder Jaffray threatened Robert with disinheritance if he refused to forsake his senseless plan of becoming a missionary.

"One fact which may have given rise to the disinheritance story was the elder Jaffray's flat refusal to finance Robert's schooling in the Missionary Training Institute. If he would consent to a compromise

---

1.   From *Grasping for Shadows*, by Wm. MacDonald. Walterick Publishers. By permission.

and enter the regular Presbyterian ministry in the Dominion, well and good. His needs would be met from the family exchequer. But Simpson! China! Never! And that was that.

"'If the Alliance sends you to China,' the father told his son, 'they'll pay every penny of the expense. Not a dime will you get from me.' Then, softening a little, 'But if you decide the whole thing was a mistake and want to come home, just let me know. I'll send you the money.'"

But that final plea had no appeal to this young stalwart. He gave himself to China for some thirty-five years.

Robert Jaffray was quite way-worn and weary on account of his exhausting and long-time missionary labors. But before he came home to retire, he gave himself to make a survey of Borneo and the Celebes of the Dutch East Indies, where some 78 million people were still without the gospel. As far as his own missionary service was concerned, Robert felt that he had done his bit, and that it was time for younger men to come and pioneer this vast, unreached, and unevangelized world where those millions were still waiting to hear.

Then God gave Robert Jaffray a strange dream.[2] He could not escape the responsibility of plunging back into this dark, untouched world to reach and rescue some of those lost souls, or else their blood would be required at his hand. And through Robert Jaffray and then his successor, Arthur Mouw (one of the writer's very personal friends), many thousands of headhunting cannibals were converted through the glorious gospel of Christ. And then, as if to crown his cross-bearing career, Robert A. Jaffray was taken captive by the Japanese and died of malnutrition in a prison camp.

Hero of God, farewell. But what shame and pity that that wealthy and unworthy father in Toronto could not say,

> Blest am I, that own for son
> Such an one.

It was the writer's privilege to know Isobel Kuhn of the China Inland Mission (now the Overseas Missionary Fellowship). Her

---

2. For details turn to the next chapter, "Woe of Missions."

mother, though a professing Christian, reacted viciously to her daughter's call to China: "Isobel, if ever you go to China, it will be over my dead body." And over her mother's dead body Isobel went to China, her mother at length admitting: "Isobel was right." But what a shame to that mother that she did not share Isobel's heavenly vision and reward!

It is a solemn fact that young people have to lead the way—often to the everlasting shame of many parents.

Henry Martyn of Cambridge set a great example for both parents and their youngsters. Here is part of Henry Martyn's own testimony:

> I can only account for my being (spiritually) stationary so long, by the intenseness with which I pursued my studies, in which I was so absorbed, that the time I gave to them seemed not to be a portion of my existence. That in which I now see I was lamentably deficient was a humble and contrite spirit, through which I should have perceived more clearly the excellency of Christ. The eagerness, too, with which I looked forward to my approaching examination for degrees, too clearly portrayed a heart not dead to the world.

When the time came for the students to enter the great Senate Chamber at Cambridge, among the crowd of young men, Martyn was alone, possibly, in the assurance, not of certain victory, but of self-abasement. A text of Scripture, upon which he had sometime before listened to a stirring discourse, was prominently in his mind: "Seekest thou great things for thyself—seek them not"; and although he had not attained to a very high maturity in Christian experience, he knew enough to steady himself by faith upon God in this critical hour.

When the result of the public debate was made known, Henry Martyn became the center of congratulating friends, for he had attained the highest honour which the University can bestow, that of senior debater of his year. At such a moment, especially when we consider in which spirit he entered the contest, we can well imagine that the color of conscious honor would flush the pale cheek of the successful student.

But from the pressing crowd of those who would rejoice with him, he seems to have turned almost sadly away, and his own words were: "*I obtained my highest wishes, but was surprised to find that I had grasped a shadow.*"

This young "saint and scholar" went to India as a missionary. Two days after his arrival in that land he wrote: "*Now to burn out for God.*" And burn out he did. No words could better describe this burning meteor-like man whose short life—he died at 31—has lighted up the shining path for many another missionary hero.

What sort of parentage had Henry Martyn? Of his earthly father we know nothing. But his spiritual heritage is most touching and enriching. Come again to Cambridge. That great scholar and preacher, Charles Simeon of the Cambridge University pulpit, while pouring forth a volume of evangelical truth, endured a most bitter portion of persecution with bricks and stones and abusive language hurled at him from college windows, and his services often disturbed by angry rioters.

For fifty to sixty years Simeon so preached the cross and lived the cross that God made him a mighty influence over the age in which he lived. And it was while the thorns of persecution were wounding him that God gave him the brilliant Henry Martyn.

When Simeon later went to view the unveiling of the portrait of the fallen missionary hero, he could only turn away to a distant part of the great hall, "crying aloud with anguish." Bystanders supposed: "That must be his father." *His father*, indeed, in a sense that none of them knew, for there was the picture of his beloved Henry, "begotten in his bonds" at Cambridge.

Blessed indeed are those fathers and mothers who like Simeon are content to forego children and houses and lands and ambitions and positions for the sake of Christ and the gospel, that they may look upon their spiritual children and say, "In Christ Jesus I have begotten you through the gospel."

For which world are we begetting our sons and our daughters? Do they not belong to him? How we should hold before them "the utmost for his highest!" And how we as parents should heed the call:

Give of your sons to bear the message glorious;
Give of your wealth to speed them on their way;
Give of yourselves, for them in prayer victorious,
And all thou givest Jesus will repay!

Trail Blazers

The *Baptist Missionary Review* once published an article on their early pioneers—"Trail Blazers"—in the field of Assam, India, in which the author said:

> The religious vocabulary of these men oftentimes seems stilted and a bit overdone to us of today. But to them life was a serious pilgrimage between two eternities. Their theology ... put backbone into them and gave them a powerfully constraining apologetic for foreign missions.
>
> They were very sure that the heathen were already damned and going to hell; they had not the slightest doubt but that all heathen religions were contraptions of Satan to hide the truth and entrap men's souls; they were very sure Jesus Christ was the only Savior of the world; they did not come to the mission field to bring about moral improvement in the lives of the heathen, nor to share mutually with Indians the truth of their respective faiths; they came to preach the unsearchable riches of Christ revealed in the gospel of the grace of God to sinners as the one hope of salvation.
>
> They preached these beliefs and lived in the power of them day by day. Missionary service to these men was a question of supreme loyalty to Jesus Christ. Flippancy had no place in their make-up. They were ambassadors for Jesus Christ. They took themselves and their work seriously.

Do we take the gospel seriously?

4

The Woe of Missions[1]

For though I preach the gospel, I have nothing to glory of: for necessity is laid upon me; yea, woe is unto me, if I preach not the gospel! (1 Corinthians 9:16).

The following letter was written by a man who originally planned to enter the Christian ministry. It appeared in *Voice* magazine of the Independent Fundamental Churches of America, November, 1957. It later appeared in our own *Prairie Overcomer* for June, 1958. May God use this challenge from a communist to awaken us, to alarm us, to shame us, and to shake us out of our indifference and ease.

What seems of first importance to you is to me either not desirable or impossible of realization. But there is one thing about which I am in dead earnest. That is, the communist cause. It is my life, my business, my religion, my hobby, my sweetheart, my wife and mistress, my bread and meat. I work at it in the daytime and dream of it at night. Its hold on me grows, not lessens, as time goes on. I'll be in it the rest of my life.

When you think of me, it is necessary to think of communism as well, because I am inseparably bound to it. Therefore I can't carry on a friendship, a love affair, or even a conversation without relation to this force which both drives and guides my life. I evaluate people, books, ideas, actions according to how they affect the communist cause and by their attitude toward it. I have already been in jail because of my ideas, and, if necessary, I'm ready to go before a firing squad.

Now, what does this mean for us communists in a personal way? Well, it means this: We are in the forefront of the working class in its titanic

---

1. This message (here slightly altered) appeared originally as a chapter in a compilation entitled *How Shall They Hear*, by Dr. M. A. Darroch of the Sudan Interior Mission, and was reprinted (by permission) in The *Prairie Overcomer*, February, 1956.

struggle with the capitalist class. We take the heaviest and most direct blows. We have a high casualty rate. We're the ones who get stoned and hanged and lynched, tarred and feathered, jailed and slandered and ridiculed, fired from our jobs and in every way made as uncomfortable as possible. A certain percentage of us get killed or imprisoned.

Even for those who escape these harsher ends of life, it's not a bed of roses. A genuine communist lives in virtual poverty. He turns back to the communist party every penny he makes above what is absolutely necessary to keep him alive.

We constantly look for places where the class struggle is the sharpest, and exploit the situation to the limit of its possibilities. We have strikes, we organize demonstrations, we speak on street corners, we fight police, we go through trying experiences many times each year which the ordinary worker has to face only once or twice in a lifetime. And when we are not doing the more exciting things, all our spare time is taken up with the dull routine chores, the endless leg work, the errands which are inescapably connected with running a live organization.

Communists don't have the time or money for many movies or concerts or t-bone steaks or decent homes and new cars. We have been described as fanatics. We are. Our lives are dominated by one great overshadowing factor, the struggle for communism.

Many leaders of the communists were schooled in the Orthodox Church in their youth. Who can blame them for their apostasy from that formal and dead orthodoxy? It is said that Khrushchev knew the four Gospels by heart. Many of these communists have the language of the Christian sanctuary. In their "consecration" to the cause of communism they have borrowed their phraseology from Christianity.

They have imitated the first-century martyrs in their dedication, in their zeal, and (often) in their poverty, all for the sake of their comrades in arms.

Another communist boasts:

We do not play with words. We are realists .... Of our salaries and wages we keep only what is strictly necessary, and give up the rest for propaganda purposes. To this propaganda we also "consecrate" all our free time and part of our holidays. You (Christians), however, give only a little time and hardly any money for the spreading of the gospel of

Christ .... Believe me, it is we who will win, for we believe in our communist message; we are ready to sacrifice everything, even our life ... but you people are afraid to soil your hands."

What is the secret of the communist's power? What fires him with the zeal of a crusader? He believes, poor deceived soul, that he has the cure for all economic ills. The fiery passion of the communists to liberate their brethren and create a new world order is built upon the belief that their mission is worth dying for. Fanaticism though it be, it is fired by faith.

Whittaker Chambers rightly said: "The communist's power is the power to hold convictions and to act upon them. Communists are that part of mankind who have recovered the power to live or die—to bear witness—for their faith." And Harold Ockenga has said: "Atheistic communism is the most aggressive force competing with Christianity. It is a missionary, crusading, materialistic religion with authoritative scriptures, inspired prophets, evangelistic methods, demand for sacrifice, and unmatched zeal. The missionary communist puts the vast number of Christians to shame."

Theirs is a faith that illustrates faith's obedience—"the obedience of faith." A faith that obeys Christ is the true Christian faith. In fact, there is no other kind of faith but the faith that obeys. Any other kind is "not another," for a "faith without works is dead"—no faith at all.

Elsewhere we refer to the deserved and drastic rebuke given the clergyman who asked the Duke of Wellington: "Does not your Grace think it almost useless and extravagant to preach the gospel to the Hindus?" The great general retorted: "What are your marching orders, sir?"

Such trifling questions as "Is world evangelization feasible?" and "Do missions pay?" betray an ignorance of the first principle of the Christian faith, namely, believing submission to the Lord Jesus Christ as the captain of our salvation. Fresh from his passion, our risen Lord said, "All *authority* is given unto me in heaven and in earth. Go ye *therefore*..." "Go ye into all the world, and preach the gospel to every creature." That command was given by the highest authority. Observe that it is no appeal to our manhood, no challenge to our dignity. Much less is it good counsel, but rather an explicit command to be implicitly obeyed.

There has been far too much emphasis on *challenge* to achievement, far too little on *obedience* to command. Failure to obey this command is to deny Christ's lordship of the church, and, in principle, to make void the whole Word of God. It is this flagrant disobedience to our "marching orders" that constitutes what has been termed "the crime of the century."

"Go ... preach"—our marching orders. "The gospel to every creature"—a plain command. Mounting millions who have never heard—a simple and terrifying fact. I say, "terrifying fact"—terrifying it should be to believers—for "these millions of unsaved souls we must confront at the bar of God. What can we do for their salvation—nay, for our own salvation from bloodguiltiness—before the sun of life shall set?" (A. T. Pierson).

This quotation from that great missionary statesman of the past generation brings into sharp focus the burden of our message, "The Woe of Missions." As disciples of Christ we are forever seeking to evade the imperative necessity of taking the gospel to the lost. Our chief wickedness, of course, is lack of submission to the lordship of Christ. We render an astounding amount of "Lord, Lord" lip service, while we do not the things which he commands.

Burning Conviction

Why has the church ceased to be militant? Where is our masculinity? Why all this effeminacy? If the church is actually a fighting force of Christian soldiers, why are we not "as an army terrible with banners"? What has killed our desire to fight? Does it come down to this, that unbelief, fatal and wicked unbelief, has killed our conviction about the absolute necessity of our message?

A distinguished church leader, as quoted by Dr. R. H. Glover, in his book, *The Bible Basis of Missions,* made the following impassioned appeal at the annual gathering of the officials of his denomination:

Why is it that the interest in foreign missions is everywhere lagging and that gifts are falling off? It is because Christian people are no longer gripped by a burning conviction that men everywhere are lost without Christ. The sense of urgency, of immediate danger, of a crisis in salvation has largely disappeared. Many of our preachers no longer preach as dying men to dying men. Our forefathers believed that men everywhere without Christ were in immediate danger of facing the wrath of God. Our modern world has largely lost this urgent note in salvation. We need to restore it… It is this loss of a mighty conviction about salvation and of both a present and a future disaster to the souls and to modern civilization without Christ that has cut the nerve of missionary obligation and enthusiasm.

Was it John Wesley who observed that nearly all error begins with false views regarding the *state*, the *need*, and the *danger* of man? The basic trouble with many today is that they are thinking outside the Book, thinking "above that which is written." For us Christians the diagnosis of the Great Physician must forever remain the last word.

The pages of divine revelation declare man to be an enemy of God, a rebel against his King, "alienated from the life of God by wicked works," rejecting the reign of the Most High, and in danger of "everlasting destruction from (i.e., proceeding from) the presence of the Lord, and from the glory of his power" (2 Thess. 1:9).

The vast and pressing need of this prodigal race is for peace, peace based upon reconciliation with God. But since God has declared that "the wages of sin is death" and that he "will by no means clear the guilty," it is evident that "without shedding of blood is no remission." In his atoning death, Christ has effected this reconciliation: "You, that were sometime alienated and enemies in your mind by wicked works, yet now hath he reconciled in the body of his flesh through death" (Col. 1:21-22). And the missionary mandate from the Director General of our campaign is to make known this reconciliation, to publish these glad tidings, to beseech men to lay down their rebellious weapons and be reconciled to the throne through the death of heaven's beloved one.

Until these great facts fasten themselves upon us, we have no gospel. If man is not an enemy, he needs no reconciliation; if not a slave, he needs no redemption; if not a sinner, he needs no forgiveness; if not dead in sins, he needs no life; if not depraved, he needs no holiness; if not polluted and filthy, he needs no cleansing.

Remedy—One and Only

If these frightful facts of man's need be so, bless God, we have the one and only gospel to meet that need. Paget Wilkes says, "It is no gospel to tell men that God merely loves good people and those that seek him. There is not even *news* in that. The *new* thing and the *good* thing of God's message is that he loves sinners; he died for rebels; he waits to show mercy on the most open-handed sinner alive. This is news indeed and good beyond reckoning."

This gospel is indeed good news, but good only to the man who gets it. Since there is "none other name under heaven given among men, whereby we must be saved," and since any man "without Christ" is "without hope and without God" in this world as well as in the world to come, it is imperative that Christ be preached to all men. Paul's argument for the universal necessity of the gospel is found in Rom. 10:14-15, where he asks these four unanswerable questions: *"How* then shall they call on him in whom they have not believed? And *how* shall they believe in him of whom they have not heard? And *how* shall they hear without a preacher? And *how* shall they preach, except they be sent?"

Woe and Bloodguiltiness

These questions help us to understand the apostle's feeling of "necessity" and "woe" when he says, *"Necessity* is laid upon me; yea, woe is unto me, if I preach not the gospel!" (1 Cor. 9:16). How urgent is this "necessity"? How serious this "woe"? Certainly Paul was overwhelmed with the urgent necessity of the gospel. As to the "woe," Paul says in another connection, "I take you to record this day, that I am pure from the blood of all men." In comment upon this passage, Lenski, the great Lutheran theologian, says:

> "Blood" is a pregnant, metonymical term for the guilt involved in bringing about death, here eternal death. On the great judgment day none of

the lost from this territory shall be able to point to Paul and say that his is the guilt. Whoever may be guilty, Paul is pure from this terrible stain.

The degree of the apostle's (and the church's) guilt involved in Paul's "Woe is unto me!" is a question only the all-wise can finally settle. But be sure he will settle it. That reckoning day is coming. However, there is little doubt that we have watered down that woe to suit our doctrinal preconceptions and to avoid our being discomforted or too seriously inconvenienced. Is it not remarkable, however, that every servant of God who has been mightily used to the winning of the lost has been fully convinced, not only of an eternal hell, but also of his own bloodguiltiness—"murder by neglect"—if he fails to deliver his message?

Men with a Woe

Listen to Hudson Taylor, that great pioneer of modern interdenominational faith missions, as he meets his personal "Woe!" God was asking him to found a new agency to carry the gospel to inland China. In his ears there rang continually these words: "If thou forbear to deliver them that are drawn unto death, and those that are ready to be slain (those slipping to the slaughter—Young); if thou sayest, Behold, we knew it not; doth not he that pondereth the heart consider it? And he that keepeth thy soul, doth not he know it? And shall not he render to every man according to his works?" (Prov. 24:11-12).

In the light of such Scriptures, Hudson Taylor says:

> The feeling of bloodguiltiness became more and more intense. Simply because I refused to ask for them, the laborers did not come forward—did not go out to China—and every day tens of thousands were passing away into Christless graves! Perishing China so filled my heart and mind that there was no rest by day, and little sleep by night, till health broke down.

He refers to this dreadful issue as a "burden so crushing—these souls, and what eternity must mean for every one of them, and what the gospel might do, would do, for all who would believe, if we would take it to them."

The final struggle came at Brighton Beach on Sunday, June 25, 1865, when, as he relates it: "Unable to bear the sight of a congregation of a thousand or more Christian people rejoicing in their own security, while millions were perishing for lack of knowledge, I wandered out on the sands alone, in great spiritual agony; and there the Lord conquered my unbelief, and I surrendered myself for this service."

Only by a complete obedience to the captain of his salvation did Hudson Taylor find relief from this confessed and awful sense of bloodguiltiness over perishing China.

Dr. A. B. Simpson expresses his awful convictions in the following song:

> A hundred thousand souls a day
> Are passing one by one away
> In Christless guilt and gloom.
> O church of Christ, what wilt thou say
> When in that awful judgment day
> They charge thee with their doom?

Let us come still nearer to our own generation and listen to the Rev. R. A. Jaffray as he relates his own God-given sense of responsibility to the "other sheep" of Borneo and the Celebes:

I am returning from a trip to Borneo and the Celebes, of the Dutch Indies, in the South Seas. The Lord has taken me to "the uttermost parts of the earth," to some of the dark places of the world, where there is no gospel light, and where, literally, "Christ is not named," for there is no one there who can name his name.

I was feeling glad after two months' absence to be returning home. I felt I had done my bit, as it were; I had obeyed his command, "Go"; I had made my report to the board, and could now settle down again to ordinary work at Wuchow, and leave the responsibility of the perishing souls I had found in these uttermost parts to others. I had done my part; the rest was with others to take up the work or not as they felt led.

But the Lord gave me a dream, one of those vivid dreams which leave a deep and lasting impression. I have seldom had such dreams in my life; but when he sends one, there is no question but that it is from him. It was a horrible dream. I thought I was at home. I was a fugitive fleeing from justice. I thought I had stains of human blood on my hands. It seemed that the Lord Jesus was pursuing me. I was full of fear and was running for my life. The pure white snow was on the ground. I stopped and tried to wash the bloodstains, the "spots of lost souls," from my hands in the snow. I looked around, and ran again. I awoke. My first words were, "Lord Jesus, what does this mean? I do not fear thee. I am not running away from thee. I have no bloodstains on my hands. I am washed clean in thy precious blood, whiter than the snow. Oh, teach me what this means. What can it mean?"

At once this Scripture came to my mind: "Son of Man, I have made thee a watchman unto the house of Israel: therefore hear the word at my mouth, and give them warning from me. When I say unto the wicked, Thou shalt surely die; and thou givest him not warning, nor speakest to warn the wicked from his wicked way, to save his life; the same wicked man shall die in his iniquity; *but his blood will I require at thine hand*" (Ezek. 3:17-18). These are the blood spots on my hands. The blood of immortal souls is required of me till I do my part to warn them, to pay my debt and preach the gospel to them. *"Necessity is laid upon me; yea, woe is unto me, if I preach not the gospel!"* (1 Cor. 9:16).

The Lord Jesus has completely cancelled the great debt of all my sins forever, but requires me to pay my gospel debt to those who have never yet heard his message of salvation. If I warn them not, if I preach not the gospel to them, their blood is required at my hands.

This great missionary leader of the Christian and Missionary Alliance absolved himself of bloodguiltiness by plunging back into the Dutch Indies and at length laying down his life in a Japanese internment camp in the Celebes. Who follows in his train?

The Rev. Guy Playfair, former General Director of the Sudan Interior Mission, expresses his own personal "Woe!" in these four lines:

> We have a blood-bought pardon;
> 'Twas purchased at infinite cost;
> That pardon left undelivered
> Leaves men eternally lost.

Missions—The Main Drive

It must be obvious from Scripture, from missionary experience, and from the history of missions that the Spirit of God is ever seeking to drive home upon our sluggish and selfish hearts the woe of missions. The Holy Spirit, the very spirit of obedience, is the spirit of missions. It is not surprising, then, that wherever a church experiences real revival there is forthwith a revival in missionary interest. We confess, therefore, that the only effective cure for this chronic disobedience to Christ's last command is a fresh impulse of divine life, and that such a revival impulse will come only through prevailing prayer and intercession.

Shall we, then, in the meantime, only pray and wait for revival? Nay, verily! Let us lay revival foundations through Bible sermons on the *Holy Spirit* and *Missions*. Let ministers and teachers press home the Spirit-filled life and the missionary message. The Bible is full of missions. Preachers and churches are biblical in proportion as they are missionary minded. But if our people are to think missions, they must be given the Bible basis of missions. Let us in our pulpits and Sunday schools not omit these messages. These O-missions have caused the fall-off in *foreign* missions and *home* missions.

Christians must become convicted and convinced that *missions is the first business of the church.* The otherwise unreached must have first place in the church's life. Missions must have first place in her thinking, first place in her giving, and first place in her going. The church must also put missions first in giving up and sending her own young people abroad.

Woe, Woe, Woe

Why should it be the exception that a young person in our family or church goes to the far-flung missionary fronts? All things being equal, that should be the rule and not the exception. In time of war the most fit of our young men go to the front. To stay at home is the exception. Who will dare to say that sin's fierce war is not being waged today on all fronts and in all its fury? Woe to the slackers! Woe to all the traitors! Woe to all draft dodgers! The fight is on, O Christian soldier! Come down out of the balconies and the bleachers and get into the thick of the fight. We must all *go*, or *let go*, or *help go*. The commander-in-chief did not say, "Stay." He said, "Go!"

Woe unto the young man who fails to go because he thinks his talents could not be fully developed and displayed in the regions beyond. What? Did their tests and trials among the lawless savages of heathendom only wither the latent powers of such men as Livingstone and Carey and Judson and Bingham and Hudson Taylor? Rather, did not those insurmountable difficulties discover and develop gifts and resources and talents that the cruelties of those countries called forth?

Woe unto those older folk who regret to see a promising young man bury himself among some benighted tribe beyond the seas. The toughest test calls for the best.

Woe unto any young man who sits waiting for a special call, as though the captain cried, "Sit still," instead of "Go!" What are your marching orders, young man?

Woe unto Christians who build up bank accounts and buy comforts to no end, instead of obeying Christ's command to send his messengers into all the world.

Woe be unto North American Christians if they forbear to deliver those of other lands who are "slipping to the slaughter!" Abraham Lincoln said, "Those who deny freedom to others deserve it not for themselves, and under a just God cannot long retain it."

> [Dare] we whose souls are lighted
> With wisdom from on high;
> [Dare] we to men benighted
> The lamp of life deny?

Woe be unto any church or denomination that builds great stately monuments of stone in this country, instead of sending the gospel to the dark parts of the earth "to win for the Lamb the reward of his sufferings." A great evangelist says: "After fifty generations, only thirty-five per cent of the people on the earth have heard the gospel …. I know of one church which spent more than $500,000 in a building program in four years. During the same time it spent only $15,000 for foreign missions."

Woe unto such a church if this awful state of affairs is not soon corrected.

Woe and Wed

What a relief when the *"woe* of missions" becomes what I would like to call the *"wed* of missions." Complete obedience, cost what it may, is better, infinitely better, than disobedience. Better a thousand times to be burdened and borne down with a great and crushing sense of responsibility for the blood of others than to seek to escape the obligations of an obedient faith.

The slavish submission of communists to their masters in Moscow shames the average Christian with such reproach that he should cry, "Woe is me for my lukewarmness to Christ." Yet how lifeless, low, and vulgar are the loyalties of the communists in comparison with the joys of complete submission to Christ. How can tribute to a tyrant ever be compared with loving response to a Redeemer? Finally, where in all communist captivity is there the joy unspeakable? The rivers of living water? The peace that passes understanding? Where in all earth's patriotisms is there a subjection comparable to the hilarious happiness of being Christ's captive, obedient unto death?

It is such a refreshing thing to listen to our own graduates—over 1,800 of them have gone abroad—as they come back on furlough from the dark places of earth, where Christ has never been named. What a joy to hear them tell of souls set free, of victories won, of trials and triumphs in the far-off lands! In spite of hardships and ageing frames, they have no complaints, but all alike have their hearts set on going back to the country of their adoption. Filled with Paul's woe, they are wedded to missions. We are reminded of the words of a prominent English divine who once said:

> There is nothing finer or more pathetic to me than the way in which missionaries unlearn the love of the old home, die to their native land, and wed their hearts to the people they have served and won; so that they cannot rest at home, but must return to lay their bones where they spent their hearts for Christ. How vulgar the common patriotisms seem beside this inverted homesickness, this passion for a kingdom that has no frontage and no favored race, the passion of a homeless Christ.

That the "woe" of missions may become indeed the "wed" of missions to the many who read these pages—is the writer's prayer.

Would You Go Back?

If you had been to heathen lands,
Where weary souls stretch out their hands
To plead, yet no one understands,
Would you go back, would you?

If you had seen the women bear
Their heavy loads, with none to share,
Had heard them weep with none to care,
Would you go back, would you?

If you had seen them in despair,
Beat their breasts and pull their hair,
While demon powers filled the air,
Would you go back, would you?

If you had seen the glorious sight,
When heathen people seeking right
Were brought from darkness into light,
Would you go back, would you?

If you had walked through Afric's sand,
Your hand within the Savior's hand,
And knew he'd called you to that land,
Would you go back, would you?

If you had seen the Christian die,
With ne'er a fear tho' death were nigh,
Had seen them smile and say goodbye,
Would you go back, would you?

Yet still they wait, a weary throng,
They've waited, some, so very long,
When shall despair be turned to song?
I'm going back, would you?

—Eva Doerksen, SIM, Nigeria

5

Roll Call and Review

THEN God intervened. He ordered the battle. As a nation God's Israel had become too dispirited, too disarmed to fight. There was not so much as one spear or shield seen "among forty thousand in Israel" (Judg. 5:8). The thought of a battle was all God's own. He knew that only by a holy war could the Israelites throw off the galling yoke of the oppressor. The Lord had sold his people "into the hand of Jabin, king of Canaan." Finally "the children of Israel cried unto the Lord: for he (Jabin) had nine hundred chariots of iron; and twenty years he mightily oppressed the children of Israel" (Judg. 4:2-3).

All this reminds us of the world's bondage and oppression at the hands of a greater than Jabin, even Satan himself. The forces of heathenism, how oppressive and cruel and powerful! "The dark places of the earth are full of the habitations of cruelty" (Psa. 74:20). Not for a mere twenty years, but for many millenniums the Devil has "mightily oppressed" many of earth's millions.

Though created in the image of God, men are sold under sin, blind and bound and bankrupt—literally oppressed and overwhelmed by the power of a nearly almighty Devil. Christ's disciples must face up to some questions: Must men (who were) created to be free men remain forever in chains? Must the enemy's oppression continue unchecked and unchallenged? Are the fortresses of the foe to be unsealed and untaken? How long shall the gates of hell hold sway over the masses of men for whom Christ died? And that all because we have failed (or refused) to believe that the deliverance of souls is no child's play, but "a battle, a real battle, not indeed with flesh and blood, but a spiritual conflict, taxing strength and nerve and heart to the uttermost" (Wilkes).

49

Turn now to God's own searching summary of his people's response to the conflict in the military crisis under Deborah and Barak. Let the reader pore over Judges 4 and 5 on his knees and catalogue himself as a volunteer for battle. If the Christian cause is indeed a conflict, a fight, a battle, war indeed, then heaven's searching review after the battle will in the day of reckoning reveal (1) the roll of honor and (2) the list of shame. And that revelation will again be, as it was under Deborah and Barak, on the basis of obedient response to military levy and of resolute service rendered in the day of battle.

The books now shut will then be open for inspection. Things long covered and concealed will suddenly be shouted from the housetops. Hidden things will be disclosed. Every secret selfishness and every unpublished sacrifice; every concealed false motive and every unknown service of love, all will come to light—"the day shall declare it" (1 Cor. 3:13).

Such a review has already been conducted. The battle call and conflict in Judges 4 and 5 are illustrative of missionary call-up and response to conflict in military terms. Under the heroic leadership of Deborah and Barak, a lot of unarmed Israelites waged a triumphant war and won a glorious victory. In a song celebrating heaven's mighty triumph, there is great honour bestowed upon certain tribes who rallied in that war, as well as great disgrace heaped upon those who drew back in the day of battle.

Let the roll of honor be the first to pass in review:

Willing Leadership

In Judges 4 we have the account of great things God had just done for Israel. Then in Judges 5 we have the celebration in song of Deborah's praise for that victory. She strikes off with a general hallelujah:

> That the leaders led in Israel,
> That the people volunteered,
> Bless the Lord! (5:2 NASB)

Then, after a few more sentences in song, Deborah returns (v. 9 NASB) to sing again of how the example set by the governors influenced many people to volunteer:

My heart goes out to the commanders of Israel,
The volunteers among the people; Bless the Lord!

Thus Deborah and Barak got their handful of ten thousand volunteers (4:6) because "the leaders took the lead in Israel." 'Tis so even till this hour. The people will "offer themselves willingly" and will hazard their lives when leaders step down from their positions of dignity and join the foot soldiers in the fight.

It still holds true that "not many wise men after the flesh, not many mighty, not many noble, are called" to this man-humbling missionary work, but there are a few like Joseph and Moses and Joshua and Othniel and Barak and Gideon and David. And in our Christian dispensation there are Paul, Chrysostom, Augustine, Luther, Calvin, Wesley, Whitefield, Knox, Carey, Livingstone, Moffat, Martyn, Brainerd, Hudson Taylor, and Robert Morrison of China. Time would fail me to tell of Mackay of Uganda, Judson of Burma, Keith Falconer of Arabia, Allen Gardiner of Tierra del Fuego, Jonathan Edwards of America, etc., etc. These men, many of them, might have been governors or prime ministers or ambassadors had not they heard the summons to a higher service. Was it not Charles H. Spurgeon who said to his son: "If God calls you to be a missionary, don't shrivel up to be a king"?

When such "leaders take the lead" in the army of the Lord, then (we repeat) many young recruits will cease to be "draft dodgers," and will follow their leaders into the thick of the fight. Oh, for more loyal and fearless leaders—men who will humbly offer themselves "willingly among the people"!

Ephraim

The first tribe for honorable mention is Ephraim: "From Ephraim those whose root is in (or against) Amalek came down" (Judg. 5:14, NASB). The Amalekites had always been against Israel (Exod. 17:15-16). They had a stronghold in Ephraim (Judg. 12:15). Therefore "Ephraim had Amalek to detain them" (Knox trans.). How could Ephraim be expected to respond for war *abroad*? They had the pressing *home* problem of warring with Amalek. Ephraim might have reasoned: "Don't talk to us about rallying recruits for a foreign invasion. Charity begins at home. We have to care for our home needs first." So Ephraim had "Amalek to detain them." But obedience to the call demanded that Ephraim should commit the care of the home front to the Lord. They boldly ventured against the more pressing foe.

There are many believers of limited vision who have never lifted up their eyes to behold the dark places of the earth so "full of the habitations of cruelty." Such Christians—who can deny that they are Christians?—use the home missionary needs as an excuse. But if we put the home front at its blackest, it is almost white beside the exceeding darkness of heathenism. Do the lesser and lower claims of the home front "detain" the reader? G. Christian Weiss rightly says: "Charity does begin at home, but charity cannot stay at home, or end at home. When charity ends at home, it is no longer charity; it becomes selfishness."

Excuses begone! Fall in line for war abroad!

> Go, *let* go, or *help* go
> 'Gainst the more oppressive foe!

Benjamin

Ephraim was the first to be mentioned with honor. But what was it that moved Ephraim to active response? "From Ephraim those whose root is in Amalek came down, following you, Benjamin, with your peoples" (Judg. 5:14, NASB). Benjamites were few in number and weak in wealth, but their leading off inspired stronger Ephraim to follow. God does not despise the day of small things. He still chooses the weak of this world. He often uses the weaker Deborahs and despised little Benjamites to get the Ephraimites to move.

We quickly forget that most of God's missionary work is done by what we would call half-rate or small people. He thus "confounds the things which are mighty."

Yet there are persons of few talents and few funds who feel too insignificant to shoulder a share in the conflict. But small gifts coupled with prevailing prayer can help mightily on most missionary fronts.

Even the children have their place in this holy war. Don't belittle the little ones. Many of God's great missionaries were called as children. So get them mustered in. They will shortly be God's leaders.

Scripture severely warns us about the servant who neglected the one talent and the one pound. Let any reader of limited gifts beware! Be inspired by little Benjamin.

Machir

"Out of Machir came down governors (commanders or lawgivers)" (Judg. 5:14). The sons of Manasseh furnished leadership. This holy war requires leaders and lawgivers and governors, men gifted with capacity to handle others for God.

Many gifted young men are led to believe that they cannot waste their many talents in the regions beyond. 'Tis the old spirit of Judas, who wonders about all "this waste" upon the Savior. What? In war do we send only the riffraff and unfit to the front? Far be it. What about General MacArthur? General Eisenhower? General Wainwright? General Montgomery? The best are none too good for this highest service.

The church folk at Antioch might easily have reasoned that Paul and Barnabas were indispensable to the home church. Doubtless there were many people in the area of Antioch who had not yet been converted. But there were more crying needs among the heathen in Asia Minor and Europe. Do we forget that the obedience of these men, and others like them, gave *us* the gospel?

The heathen world has claimed some of the greatest missionary characters, some of whom we have already mentioned, men who might have become great industrialists, renowned statesmen, military heroes, but who answered the call to a nobler ambition. Consider the missionary in China who was approached by an oil company to represent that multi-million-dollar concern in the Orient. A good salary was offered, but instantly refused. The salary was stepped up, and up, and up until finally the representative asked, "Whatever is the matter, is the salary not big enough?" To which the noble missionary hero replied, "The salary is plenty, in fact too much, but the job isn't big enough."

Zebulun and Naphtali

"Out of Zebulun they that handle the pen of the writer" (Judg. 5:14 and 4:6). Out of Zebulun and Naphtali come two classes of militants:

1. There were those who "handle the pen of the writer," those who performed the work of the scribe. They were clerks who published orders, wrote letters, mustered in recruits, kept records and accounts. These were better skilled as secretaries than in the arts of war. This work may seem not so exciting as front-line service, but some of the great missionary heroes and heroines are hidden in home offices, in missionary headquarters, in churches, in Bible schools and mission schools. They are writing letters, interviewing candidates, recruiting soldiers for Christ, keeping the books, and rendering accounts.

Such persons are classed with the most brilliant front-line fighters of the campaign. Let no young man or woman despise his gift or bury his talent. Every man must, "according as he has received the gift, minister the same." "To each man his work"—all for the glory of God.

Thus, for soldiers under the captaincy of Christ, David's agelong principle of reward obtains: "As his part is that goeth down to the battle, so shall his part be that tarrieth by the stuff: they shall part alike" (1 Sam. 30:24). Share alike in the day of rewards; yes, "part alike" *if* they share and sacrifice on the home front as the missionary sacrifices on the foreign front.

2. Some men of Zebulun and Naphtali, though better skilled in books than in the arts of war, quit their desks and took to the field of battle.

> The scribes of Zebulun
> and learned men,
> To wield the sword,
> laid down the pen.

These tribes were the most bold and daring of Barak's forces. "Zebulun and Naphtali were a people that jeoparded their lives unto the death in the high places of the field (Judg. 5:18). As fearless fighters they "could set the battle in array … and were not of a double heart" (1 Chron. 12:33 ASV). With single-hearted heroism they faced Jabin's 900 chariots of iron, despising danger, defying even death itself in so good and great a cause. "Better die in honor than live in bondage" (Henry).

The mission field still demands men and women like Epaphroditus, who, "for the work of Christ came nigh unto death, hazarding his life" (Phil. 2:30 ASV). Thank God for such young heroes as our own Phil Masters (class of '59), who not only hazarded his life, but lost it as he ventured into that untouched tribe. And all honor to Chester Burke of our Prairie staff, whose life was snuffed out by the Simbas of the Congo. For such men death has no terrors if only they may "win for the Lamb the reward of his sufferings."

Issachar

"And the princes of Issachar were with Deborah; as was Issachar, so was Barak; into the valley they rushed forth at his feet" (Judg. 5:15 ASV). The children of Issachar "were men that had understanding of the times, to know what Israel ought to do" (1 Chron. 12:32 ASV). These princes constituted a council of war-advisers. But did Barak go on foot into the valley, into the place of great danger? Then "into the valley they rushed forth at his feet." Along with Barak the princes of Issachar became foot soldiers with him, forgetting their honor and ease, and exposing themselves with him on the field of battle. Their motto was "Whither thou goest I will go."

What mighty motive power such a commitment contains when said to the Captain of our great missionary campaign! "Anywhere with Jesus"—anything, any time—yea, "anywhere, provided it be forward." Whether it be to do, to dare, to die, let us always be "at his feet."

> In his heart;
> In his hand;
> At his feet;
> At his command!

The mission field still needs a host of foot soldiers. Editor David Lawrence once said regarding military victory: "Fighting men will remain the final key to victory in tomorrow's warfare." And he was thinking of the common foot soldier. Mission leaders have found that the call for specialists with skill has led many young men of few talents to feel unneeded and unwanted on the mission field. That call for skilled men has been overdone. Again the call comes for foot soldiers. And again God will take the "things which are not to bring to nought the things that are."

The List of Shame

So much for those tribes written on the roll of honor. Next comes the searching out of the list of shame.

Reuben

Poor Reuben, still "as unstable as water." Note how he is censured: "By the water courses of Reuben there were great resolves of heart. Why sattest thou among the sheep folds, to hear the pipings for the flocks? At the water courses of Reuben there were great resolves of heart" (Judg. 5:15-16 ASV).

The alarm of war had sounded. The Reubenites heard the summons to arms. They were stirred by the bugle blast. And theirs was no shallow-pan interest. Their response was sympathetic, promising, inspiring. They thrilled with patriotic impulse.

Twice over in these verses it is said that "by the water courses of Reuben there were great resolves of heart ... great searchings of heart." Various are other translations of the emotional reactions of Reuben: "great thoughts of heart," "great debates of heart," "great impressions of heart," "great decrees of heart," "great decisions of heart," "great enactments of heart," "great counselings of heart."

Yes, the Reubenites were stirred by the call to arms. The situation was desperate. The enemy had "mightily oppressed" them for twenty years. Had they not experienced enough bondage and pain and misery to set them on the warpath? How could they be callous to so urgent a call? The summons to duty was clear, unmistakable, challenging. Their response was hearty. Instant was their reaction. They believed: "Where duty calls or danger, be never wanting there."

Reuben's men, however, were a careful and calculating lot of fellows. As they thought things over and discussed the dangers—"great were their debatings"—they had many counselings and great searchings of heart. Perhaps some bright ideas came to them. Who knows, may this battle call be only that of a misguided and emotional Deborah? What! Just a woman! What has a woman to do with war? And a woman leader—how unscriptural! And then Barak must not be much of a man to follow a mere woman. The whole venture seems a bit unorthodox. And to think of our few unarmed men daring to go against the mighty Sisera with his 900 chariots of iron! Preposterous!

Amidst their many deliberations and considerations, there came the call of comforts and cash. They felt the pull of the purse strings. And how strong came the call from the sheep folds! But there thunders Deborah's heart-searching interrogation: "Why sattest thou among the sheep folds, to hear the pipings for the flocks?" (ASV) Why? Business was good. How beautiful sounded the "bleatings of the sheep"! Of course they still had great heart searchings and resolutions—to volunteer, to go, and to win a war. But they listened to the pipings for the flocks, to the call of business, to the peaceful shepherd songs. The trumpet call to fight faded away. "The sound of the flute seemed so much sweeter than the battle bugle" (Weiss).

How much this sounds like the young enthusiast of today, the man God calls to share in the Christian warfare, and to carve out a kingdom on foreign shores! He hears the bugle call. Perhaps he stands up in the meeting and volunteers. He may suffer many struggles and debates and great searchings of heart. He may undergo mental wrestlings and inward agonies and emotional pains.

Am I describing some young reader? One minute you are impelled to go. Then comes the call of home and friends and comfort. One such young man has recently left my office to go back home. We held solemn counselings and discussions and debatings. Finally he confessed to the backward call: "I am going to get a job and make some money and get married—as soon as my young lady has finished her schooling."

Another case. A splendid Christian woman, young and beautiful and well saved, left our missionary conference (and the call of God) with the sigh: "I am torn between this call and the young man I want to marry." Back she goes, perhaps to wade through seas of trouble to her own shameful undoing.

Young man, are you suffering some of these serious heart searchings and inner struggles? "Seekest thou great things for thyself?" while heroic young women forsake all to go out and pioneer in mission fields that cry out for men? You hear the summons to fight, but you have a good office job, a promising career, a bright business prospect. Of course you prefer to push the pencil rather than push the battle.

Or you may be a young farmer. You hear the chug of the tractor, the music of the machines, the grunt of the pigs, the bleating of the sheep. The call of the cattle is louder than the call to battle. Perhaps your big, bulging bank account blocks your road to blessing. The love of money is the root of many forms of evil. Maybe your ambition is for a teaching position, or politics, or some other legitimate business. "I'll make money to give to missions." That may be what God purposes for some persons. But if God wants you on the foreign field, there can be no substitute for obedience—"no substitute for victory" (MacArthur).

You may experience periodical wakenings, enthusiastic kindlings, great heart searchings, deep soul stirrings. It is very possible to have great impressions of heart and make great resolutions while still sitting in the bleachers, or in the "comfortable pew." Your sluggish response is: "Here am I—yea, *still here.*" Have you ever brought yourself to cry out, *"Send me"?* You can have great heart agonies, shed many tears, make good resolutions, but, after all, fail to move out. Willing, but not moving. Willing is not enough. Get going. How frightful to consider that at the coming battle review your career may be summed up in three words: *"Stirred,* but *Stayed"!* (Weiss).

Gilead

Gilead abode beyond Jordan (Judges 5:17).

The Gileadites were not merely sluggish. Theirs was a godless insensibility, a guilty indifference. Why cross Jordan? Why go so far? Maybe the need is not so urgent. In any case this is no forced call, no draft. We are under no obligation to make such a move. Besides, Jordan separates us from the battlefield. If it is purely a matter of option with us, we prefer to run no risk. Why rush headlong into danger?

The missionary cause meets with similar insensibility and indifference. Why cross the water? Why go to such lengths? After all, the heathen are far across the sea. That is their world. They have their own religions. Why create a religious riot? They prefer to be left alone. They may be ignorant, but they are contented as they are. Why disturb them?

Ours becomes murder by neglect. "Am I my brother's keeper?" Thus we hush the call, quench the Spirit, turn "draft dodgers"—and some day we shall have to answer for our downright disobedience.

Dan

"And Dan, why did he remain in ships?" (Judg. 5:17 ASV) Why? Business was booming. Dan was too busy making money. In fact, war made shipping better. And didn't the country have need of a good mercantile balance?

The call of commerce can easily kill the call of Christ. So often we hear the reasoning: "You know, the economy needs businessmen and teachers and doctors and nurses." And it gets them. God can go without. And the heathen world can do without.

It mattered little to Dan that the cause of their captive people brought disgrace and blasphemy to the name of the Lord. Dan could not leave his ships. The Lord's cause demanded that Dan turn his back on the affairs of this life and make the Lord's battle his first business. Did Dan not realize this? O Dan, awake thou that sleepest! Your ships will sooner or later suffer shipwreck.

Hearken, O Christian man still under the spell of some supreme attraction of the world. Do you not know that the day must come when you and your darling idols will have to part? You may be a good-living Christian man, but "what profit on your dying bed to remember that you have labored here for that which you cannot carry with you? You have enlarged your barns, increased your merchandise, raised your family, and left your children in prosperity; and now the sentence falls upon your trembling soul, 'Give an account of thy stewardship, for thou mayest be no longer steward'" (W. Hay Aitken).

Asher

He preferred the ease and comfort of his seaside resort. "Asher sat still at the haven of the sea, and abode by his creeks (Judg. 5:17 ASV). Had Asher become so accustomed to a "plush" life that he could not consider the difficulty, the danger, the hardship of war? "The prosperity of fools shall destroy them" (Prov. 1:32).

Will God have to allow the communists to "knock the complacency out of us" to get us totally committed to "greatest effort, utmost unselfishness, infinite pains, capacity for self-sacrifice"—for *his sake?*

Asher could not leave his comfortable cottage on the Mediterranean. He "sat still at the haven of the sea."The mention of this craven comfort-loving tribe is concluded with a fresh outburst of commendation of Zebulun and Naphtali: "Zebulun was a people who despised their lives even to death. And Naphtali also, on the high places of the field" (Judg. 5:18, NASB).

Our affluence has well-nigh nullified any semblance of Christian soldiery. The pastor of a certain church was asked how it was that his church had so much more to give to missions. Note his reply: "The people of this church have decided that a lot of modern gadgets and things are not necessary, so they have more money for missions."Nor have they a lot of cottages by the lake to consume their cash and their concern. The modern mania of this gadget-loving generation—for a hundred unnecessary things—well, how *can* God's cause prosper while we are swept along with the tide of spending and indulgence?

Meroz

"Curse ye Meroz, said the angel of the Lord; curse ye bitterly the inhabitants thereof; because they came not to the help of the Lord, to the help of the Lord against the mighty" (Judg. 5:23). Of what was Meroz guilty?—merely the omission of plain and positive duty. They did not join up on the side of the enemy. Far be it! They only refused to help the people of God. They lived less than ten miles from Barak's home. Theirs was the sin of undone duty, the sin of omission. It might be well said that with God's people the sins of omission are greater than the sins of commission.

Do I forget that it can be a crime to be a Christian—if I fail to respond to the responsibility of the Christian call-up? I can be cursed for inaction in a crisis.

A vessel was stranded near the harbor amidst the raging storm at sea. Some seventy souls were imperiled. There drew into the harbor an old sea captain with a seaworthy ship. He could have lent help, but he reasoned that the people in jeopardy would somehow make it to land. So he tucked himself away for the night and enjoyed a comfortable sleep.

The next morning the folk on shore took notice of the anchored craft yonder in the harbor and they made inquiry. They brought the old captain to land and held "kangaroo court," charging him with responsibility for the death of those seventy drownings.

The old captain protested: "Gentlemen, I protest your decision, for I have had nothing whatsoever to do with the death of these people."

To this the court responded: "That is just your crime, sir; you could have done something, but you didn't. 'Tis not for what you did that we condemn you, but for what you failed to do." And they hanged him—for undone duty.

May I muse a moment with my reader? Suppose I, like the men of Meroz, live nearby the needy battlefield. Barak's home was but

7½ miles from Meroz. Any missionary front is now but a few hours away. So you and I do live nearby. And the war is on. You and I have heard the summons. *There* is the field, *there* is the foe, *there* is the fight.

I know that *there*, over *there*, men die without Christ. I cannot plead ignorance. I could help, I could lend a hand, I could easily contribute. If unable to go myself, I could with my brethren, send that missionary. That ready recruit is stalled—stalled for only one reason, for the lack of the help I might give. Dare I do nothing?

Would the "angel of the Lord" again cry, "Curse ye, those Christian men of Meroz"—and of many churches—"curse ye bitterly the inhabitants thereof; because they came not to the help of the Lord, to the help of the Lord against the mighty"? How bitter are the blight and the barrenness and the curse that befall men with undone duty!

Oh, for the ear to hear the trumpet blast calling us to arms! Jeremiah cried, "I cannot hold my peace, because thou hast heard, O my soul, the sound of the trumpet, the alarm of war" (Jer. 4:19).

What shall be our response to God's military call-up? The grand review will one day reveal the roll of honor and the list of shame. In which list shall I appear? Horrible to contemplate:

> Shall I be but another name
> Added to the list of shame?

The following is a condensed account as told during our annual Missionary Conference by the Rev. J. B. Toews of the Mennonite Brethren.

Pete was well aware of the intense suffering of his other brothers and sisters back in the Ukraine. He had managed to get over to America and to settle in Minnesota. There his business flourished, and he regularly corresponded with George back in Russia, and regularly sent sufficient funds to keep his brothers and sisters from starving. Yet, in spite of all that he sent, one by one each passed away, until only George was left. At length this surviving brother escaped from Russia and made his way to America. He did not come all the way to Minnesota but settled in Wisconsin.

There was little correspondence between the two brothers, Pete feeling that there was something unaccountable about the curtain that seemed to have fallen over the departure of his brothers and sisters. It came to pass that George fell ill and Pete went down to Wisconsin to see him. He found him sick in the hospital. After some little conversation Pete finally inquired: "George, what was the matter? Didn't I send enough to keep them all alive?"

George offered some possible explanations until at length he came out with it: "Oh, Pete, you sent enough, but I kept it for myself."

George had been guilty of the crime of covetousness—murder by confiscation. And George himself shortly died in the hospital, killed by his conscience. His "sin had found him out." 'Twas the cost of disobedience.

6

The Cost of Disobedience (1)
or Sin Finding Us Out[1]

Sadhu Sundar Singh was once travelling in the mountains with a Tibetan companion on a bitterly cold day when snow was falling. Both men were so nearly frozen to death that they despaired of arriving at their destination alive. About that time they stumbled over a man half buried in the snow, unconscious and nearly dead from exposure. The Sadhu suggested that they carry the unfortunate man to shelter, but the Tibetan refused to help, insisting that they would have all that they could do to save themselves.

While the Tibetan passed on his way, the Sadhu shouldered the man and with great difficulty managed to struggle on with his heavy burden. Through his extra exertion Sundar began to warm up, and before long the nearly frozen fellow hanging on his shoulders began to share his warmth. Soon the Sadhu came upon the body of the Tibetan, frozen to death. By the time Sundar had arrived at the village, the half-dead man had recovered consciousness. With a full heart Sundar thought of the words of his master: "Whosoever will save his life shall lose it: and whosoever will lose his life for my sake shall find it."

A Law Inexorable

This experience of Sundar Singh perfectly illustrates the principle that he who loves his life and selfishly saves it will lose it. To be self-centred is to be self-destroyed. "Myself, arch-traitor to myself." Self carries within itself the element of its own destruction. When I

---

1. From *Crowded to Christ* by L. E. Maxwell, Moody Press, Moody Bible Institute of Chicago, 1976. Used by permission.

think of my family, my home, my cash, my church, my denomination, my little kingdom, in terms of self—whatever constitutes my life, its enjoyment and end—that is spiritual suicide. It is law, law in its very essence, law inexorable, that the preservation of self is the surest path to self-destruction. On the contrary, the law of love, which is "the law of Christ," is to forfeit life, to lay it down, to lose it. To deny this working principle is to deny the very foundation of our salvation. When Jesus faced the cross, he said he *must* go, *must* suffer, *must* be killed. In that *"must"* was embodied love's law, a principle inevitable, abiding, ageless.

The words cast at Christ on the cross, "He saved others; himself he cannot save," express the profoundest truth. In order to save us he must stay there on the cross, *must* die. He could not save himself and others. Nor was this principle of laying down his life confined to his death. His was a *life* of poverty. He was poor, very poor; not merely "poor in spirit," but *literally poor*.

Indeed his whole life, from the filthy stable at his birth to the borrowed tomb at his death, was one of privation, weakness, sorrow, suffering, one of spending and being spent for others. The only way he could save men, whether in life or in death, was by the sacrifice of himself—"He saved others; himself he cannot save." He recognized it as the very principle of life, as heaven's own law of propagation: "Verily, verily, I say unto you, Except a corn of wheat fall into the ground and die, it abideth alone: but if it die, it bringeth forth much fruit. He that loveth his life shall lose it; and he that hateth his life in this world shall keep it unto life eternal" (John 12:24-25).

A missionary tells of his boyhood days back in Wisconsin when the family was pursued by that wolf—hunger. His old father brought out of the cellar the few potatoes that were left and said, "Mother, we've got to plant these." Mother cried, "Daddy, we just can't do it; we'll have nothing to eat." But the father insisted. The mother stood there with tears streaming down her cheeks as she saw those few potatoes being cut to pieces and buried in the ground.

In the fall, however, there was a great ingathering of potatoes—food for many days. His mother would have kept them and consumed them—and starved, possibly. His father lost them to find them again, find them all new and multiplied.

The lesson is plain. We parents, as well as our children, need to be taken right out of our personal cellar, taken out of the darkness of a self-centred life—perhaps out of cold storage—and cut into a thousand pieces and planted and exposed to the disintegrating forces of death. Such is God's only law of multiplication. We cannot improve on heaven's "corn-of-wheat" program.

> The corn of wheat to multiply
> Must fall into the ground and die.

Reuben and Gad Forewarned

Our obedience to this law is not only the one imperative for multiplication, but also our only assurance of personal safety and survival. A crisis in Israel's early history vividly illustrates this fact. The nation was about to enter upon the conquest of Canaan and take possession of that land. She had already taken the territory on the east side of Jordan. On the west side of the river lay the promised land challenging conquest, for it was full of Israel's enemies.

Then there arose a question, a problem, a crisis. Two of their tribes, Reuben and Gad, possessed great herds of cattle, and therefore requested that they might settle down on the already conquered pasture land east of Jordan.

But the other tribes had not yet been brought into their territory and inheritance; Palestine proper had yet to be conquered and divided among the other ten tribes. Moses therefore sternly rebuked Reuben and Gad, warning them that if they failed to go across Jordan with the others they would not only incur the anger of the Most High but also "destroy *all* the people," including themselves. At length the two tribes consented to go over and fight on until all the people had come to their God-given inheritance. Here was their reply: "We ourselves will go ready armed … until we have brought them unto their place …. We will not return unto our houses, until the children of Israel have inherited every man his inheritance" (Num. 32:17-18).

The two tribes thus agreed that they would neither rest nor settle down until every man had come into his possession. The agreement satisfied the divine demand, and Moses' word of assurance to them was: "Afterward ye shall return, and be guiltless before the Lord, and before Israel; and this land [east of Jordan] shall be your possession before the Lord. But if ye will not do so, behold, ye have sinned against the Lord: and *be sure your sin will find you out*" (32:22-23).

These two tribes learned that day that their only personal safety and their only assurance of possessing their own possessions lay in their first bringing the rest of Israel into their promised inheritance. They were furthermore warned that any failure to do so would mean that they had "sinned against the Lord." Concerning such sin and its consequences they were not left in the dark: *"Be sure your sin will find you out."* What a solemn warning for God's people! This passage is commonly taken to apply only to sinners, but in its immediate context it has to do with the failure of God's people to bring others into the land of promise, the sin and consequence of omitting known duty.

Herein lies the most profound principle of missions. If we fail to "go armed before the Lord to war," as Israel was bidden to do, until we win the lost of other nations and bring them into their inheritance and into their possessions in Christ, then the word of warning still applies: "If ye will not do so, behold, ye have sinned against the Lord: and *be sure your sin will find you out.*"

Results of Disobedience

History teems with instances of churches which, when faced with obedience to the spirit of missions, refused to go forward—and died. North Africa was once ablaze with gospel light, but the church of those areas took to controversy, instead of taking territory farther inland. She failed to bring Africa's unreached millions to their gospel possessions. For this criminal neglect Christ removed her candlestick. Having lost her savor, she was trodden under foot by the Muslim scourge. Her sin found her out.

Think, too, of the Armenian Christians. How miserably they failed to take the gospel to the Turks! They spared themselves the pains and sacrifices necessary to go to their cruel neighbors and win them for Christ. For this omission of duty they brought upon themselves from those very Turks an unspeakable baptism of blood, a virtual extinction. Their sin found them out.

Coming closer home, we may note how Ontario Christians have not carried Christ to nearby Quebec, that great mission field always lying right at their door. Now Ontario is being taken over by the Catholics. Be sure, Ontario, your sin will find you out. Such is the law of retribution—retroactive and righteous. If this is indeed the law of life, and especially of church life, when will the church obediently believe it?

We turn to more easily perceived and vivid experiences for concrete illustration of this law. Before World War II many Christian parents had been reluctant to surrender their boys to go to the missionary fronts and capture men for Christ; but the government wrung from them and their sons an obedience which hitherto they had refused to yield to the captain of their salvation.

Instead of going abroad voluntarily to carry the good news to needy neighbors—we are thinking of Japan especially—these very sons were compelled in self-defense to carry death and destruction to these very nations. Many such soldiers—all thanks to their heroic sacrifices on our behalf—seemed to be little more than fodder for foreign guns. Were those guns but the backfire of disobedience, the disobedience of some of those Christian soldiers to an earlier and higher summons?

Failure to abide by these principles of gospel propagation has been the source of untold national woes, as well as the cause of our own moral deterioration and spiritual death. Subsequent to the war, the American Baptist Foreign Missionary Society published a frank acknowledgment of its own fall-off in foreign missions, admitting therein: "We have taken the war seriously. We have all but ignored the program which, if we had taken it seriously, would have made the war impossible."

Export—Or Die

Concerning the one business of the church, somebody says, "It is evangelize or fossilize." Government leaders know that their whole financial power and life depend upon the amount of business done abroad. The motto therefore of many nations today is: "Export—or Die."

Herein the children of this world are again demonstrated to be "wiser than the children of light," for to the Christian church there is no surer road to bankruptcy and ruin than to fail to export. Our spiritual assets and reserves are only in the proportion that we get our gospel goods abroad. "There is that scattereth, and yet increaseth; and there is that withholdeth more than is meet, but it tendeth to poverty" (Prov. 11:24). The nations are only acting on gospel and missionary principle when they adopt the slogan, "Export—or Die."

This principle finds illustration all around us. Modern warfare makes it necessary that leading nations exercise vigilance as to their outposts, their advance air bases, their military missions. This is their first and highest kind of military strategy. America knows, we are told, that her only safety at home lies in advancing her military missions abroad.

Herein lies a lesson for the church. Instead of retrenching and recalling our missionaries (thinking thereby to save our failing budget, save our home churches, save our denominational lives), we should still keep the frontiers manned and press on into farther untaken territory. Our only safety at home lies in advancing our missions abroad. Foreign missions is not only our supreme obligation, but also (and for that very reason) our highest form of divine strategy.

In view of these vital principles of law and life and multiplication, how must fundamental churches face the crying need of a thousand million still shrouded in darkness? Many orthodox groups are full of splendid people, old as well as young, who need to "lose," i.e., lay down, their lives. If the corn-of-wheat program is not followed, those churches will soon become like great granaries full of musty, mouldy, worm-eaten wheat—unplanted grain. For very survival as well as for fruitfulness, they must send forth their young people to light up the regions beyond, lest their own light be turned into darkness—"and how great is that darkness!"

As I write, the news media are hot with strategy reports on how best to get the oil transported from northern Canada and Alaska to the oil-hungry markets of the world. What is this oil for but to light up and warm up and build up, not only Canada but other lands as well? The church is shamed again and again by men of the world, who for mere gain will obediently brave all manner of hardship to land their goods on foreign shores.

"The sons of this world are for their own generation wiser than the sons of light" (Luke 16:8 ASV). Behold how money-loving men of Canada's wheat belt are bent on getting their grain—the gain of grain—to the food-hungry millions in foreign lands. Some 800 million bushels of Canadian grain were shipped to foreign shores in one year. An advertisement for the Canadian National Railway in *Time* states:

> It wasn't easy. It only happened because everybody—the farmers, the grain-elevator agents, the grain companies and cooperatives, the railways and other shipping companies, the port terminals and the Wheat Board—everybody involved worked long, hard, and against tremendous odds to make it happen.

The ad carried this significant caption: "Canadian grain has a world market. The challenge is to get it there." But how was it gotten there? One only need to recall how all the news media were for many months questioning, wondering, prodding, charging any and every agency involved in any way with grain transportation—"to *get it there.*"

Need we say that there is a famine for the Word of God—in every foreign land? Let us not cease to prod and to provoke God's people to get the gospel moving to the famine-stricken countries—"to *get it there.*"

"A missionary writing from Manchuria," says Dr. Glover, "told of seeing displayed by a Standard Oil depot in that faraway country the ambitious slogan: 'Get the light to every dark corner of the world.'" What better slogan for Christ's disciples?

Abraham Lincoln, the great emancipator, is reported to have said: "Those who deny freedom to others deserve it not for themselves, and, under a just God, cannot long retain it." On more than one occasion Jesus laid down this principle concerning the use and abuse of gospel gifts and privileges: "For whosoever hath (made gain), to him shall be given (still more to invest), and he shall have more abundance: but whosoever hath not (made gain), from him shall be taken away even that he hath." It is as though he had said: Make gain with your spiritual gifts, your earthly riches, your gospel freedoms—pass them on to others. Use them, or lose them—it is divine law.

> Shall we whose souls are lighted
> With wisdom from on high,
> Shall we to men benighted
> The lamp of life deny?

For Christ and the World

A communist has for his motto, "Communism for all, and my all for communism." Until the church of Jesus Christ regains that first love for Christ that constrained the early disciples to live and die for Christ, to sacrifice all for the sake of his dear name, and to go into all the world preaching the gospel, we stand condemned by this child of his generation. Oh, that we all might say in truth, "Christ for all, and my all for Christ."

How true the charge of Alexander Duff that the Church is playing at missions. How are we to explain that after nineteen centuries the world is still not reached by the gospel? What shall we say on that solemn day of judgment? *What excuse shall we give?* That we were not commanded to go into all the world? That we did not know? That we did not have the means to go?

7

The Cost of Disobedience (2)
"We are forever seeking some excuse"

One would suppose that nothing more is needed to make us move than the marching orders, the plain, explicit, oft-repeated command of Christ's "Go ye." The spirit of missions is simply the spirit of obedience to this command.

However, in spite of all we have said about our sin finding us out, there may be those who, in some form or another and perhaps all unconsciously, have hold of a darling little lie or alibi by which they excuse themselves from their missionary obligations. Certain subtle reasonings have crept in which kill a sense of responsibility and cut the nerve of missionary endeavor. Let us examine some of these alibis.

Doorway of Ignorance

(1) *Many Christians hold to the false hope that the heathen are not lost, because they have never heard the gospel.* It is said that a student once asked Charles Spurgeon if he thought the heathen who had never heard the gospel would be saved. He answered, "It is more of a question with me whether we, who have had the gospel and fail to give it to those who have it not, can be saved." It has been the writer's personal conviction that it is not so much a question of what God is going to do with the heathen who have not heard as it is a question of how he will adjudicate upon saints who have disobeyed more light than the heathen have ever had, and who with such amazing privileges have trampled them under foot.

If for the heathen the entrance into heaven be through the doorway of ignorance, then it would indeed be folly for them to be wise.

In fact, were that so, the only reason millions on *this* continent are lost would be that they have heard the gospel. The fact is the heathen are lost, not because they have not heard the gospel, but because of known light, the light of *conscience* and *creation*, that they have disobeyed. Anyone reading Romans, chapters 1 and 2, can see that the heathen are consciously under "wrath" and "without excuse."

The great missionary leader, Dr. A. B. Simpson, founder of the Christian and Missionary Alliance, has declared:

> The heathen pass out of wretched existence here into a darker future beyond. Do you say you do not believe this—that God is too merciful to let them be lost, and that there must be some other way of hope and salvation for them?
>
> Beloved, this settled unbelief of God's Word is probably the secret of most of our sinful neglect of the heathen world. We are pillowing our conscience on a lie. God has solemnly told us in his Word that there is no other name under heaven given among men whereby we must be saved, but the name of Jesus. The tenderest voice that ever spake on earth declared, "except a man be born again, he cannot enter into the kingdom of God." If God could have saved men in any easier way, he would never have given his Son to the horrors of Calvary.

The question actually comes down to this: Shall I charge the Son of God with the unbelievable and unparalleled folly of having come all the way from heaven's glory to be made sin and die under the wrath of the offended holiness, to save from outer darkness and damnation a people in no danger of ever going there? Shall I further charge the risen Christ, who urged his apostles and disciples to go and preach this gospel to every creature, with ignorance of the uncondemned condition of the heathen? Finally, was that greatest of all missionaries only self-deceived when, in his zeal for lost men everywhere, he cried, "Woe is unto me, if I preach not the gospel"?

Surely it is unnecessary to dwell longer upon this error. Let any man read his Bible in subjection to its plain declarations regarding the lost, and he will know that men without Christ are without God and without hope, either in this world or in the world to come.

One of our own graduates, Earl Carlson, was bitten as a young Christian with the false hope that the heathen would be saved because they had not heard. When, under the providence of God, he was later laboring with Filipinos in Alaska, he said to himself: "Now these are the men who have never heard the gospel; they will therefore go to heaven when they die."

Before long, however, he came to the conclusion that if these were the men who were going to heaven he did not want to go there. His simple conclusion—one he might easily have reached had he read his Bible aright—was that sinful men are not fit for God's holy presence. He was converted at once to what the Scripture says about the lost condition of the heathen.

Mr. Carlson early burned out for God among the hill tribes of China. A worthy pioneer of that land said of this young man, "A better missionary than Earl Carlson never went to any foreign land." However, unless he had become convinced of the lostness of the heathen, he would have made no missionary worthy of the name.

(2) Another subtle insinuation, voiced by some otherwise fundamental missionaries, is this: *God knows who would have accepted the gospel had they heard it, and he will therefore save all whom he has foreseen.* On this presumption, why the insistence of Christ and the apostles of getting to the heathen with the glorious message? Why go into any part of the world if the foreknowledge of God will take care of the whole problem? This reasoning calls for further treatment.

No Second Chance

(3) Another error which has gained some currency among orthodox believers, manifestly among those inclined to evade their responsibilities to missions, is the assumption that *the heathen, whether at home or abroad, will be given a second chance, and that Christ will hereafter be proclaimed to all such.* This belief is based upon what seems to be a twisted view of one portion of Scripture. We believe that the much-disputed passage, 1 Peter 3:18–4:6, refers not to the preaching made by Christ to people after death, but to the time when "the longsuffering of God waited in the days of Noah, while the ark was a-preparing."

This is manifestly the sense of 4:6 where those "that are (now) dead," having had the gospel preached to them during their lifetime, will be "judged according to men in the flesh." Noah was "a preacher of righteousness" (2 Pet. 2:5), and Peter informs us that it was "in the spirit" with resurrection power that Christ "preached" through Noah to the men who are now "spirits in prison" awaiting judgment. Only those who lack the spirit and "woe" of missions can be content to leave the eternal destinies of lost men to an assumed after-death preaching of the gospel.

Certainly the general teaching and tone of all Scripture is that man's state after death is fixed, final, irreversible. The rich man in hell was told of "a great gulf fixed" and impassable. Believers are to exhort others daily "while it is called Today" (Heb. 3:13). How plain is the warning that "Whatsoever a man soweth [in time], that shall he also reap [in eternity]"! Nor does the Scripture say "after death a second chance," but, rather, "after this the judgment" (Heb. 9:27). Where is there any Scripture proof of probation and second chance after death? Surely the present life determines the final and fixed state of every man. "In the place where the tree falleth, there it shall be" (Eccles. 11:3). So Judas went "to his own place." John's last word seems conclusive: "He that is unjust, let him be unjust still: and he which is filthy, let him be filthy still: and he that is righteous, let him be righteous still: and he that is holy, let him be holy still" (Rev. 22:11).

If there be no positive danger of endless punishment awaiting those who die out of Christ—certainly there is no salvation apart from Christ—then our gospel is neither imperative nor necessary. The inexpressible gravity of our message cannot be vindicated apart from the positive danger of eternal woe. That the missionary nerve has been severed among those who fail in these convictions is manifest by the poverty of missionary effort among all such. (We are not here dealing with false sects which manifest a fleshly zeal "not according to knowledge." Nor are we discussing the varying degrees of punishment according to light and opportunity as in Rom. 2:11–15.)

Not Angels—But Men

(4) Other orthodox leaders are heard to say: *"Had God chosen the angels to evangelize the world, heaven would have been emptied in five minutes; but for some strange reason he has not been pleased to employ them to do this missionary work."* We do not presume to know aught of Heaven's reasons for so ordering this missionary program, neither dare we imply that God has arbitrarily—"for some strange reason"—given us the privilege (privilege verily it is, and a glorious one) of doing this task, whereas he might have chosen any one of several, and possibly better, methods.

Certainly the tone of all Scripture is to the effect that Christ has not only commanded us, but that he is also *shut up to his own redeemed people,* those who know salvation's story, to carry out world-wide evangelization.[1] If it were only for some strange reason, presumably whimsical and arbitrary on God's part, that he has chosen us to do such holy work, then I would at once begin to feel that I need not become too much concerned, much less "beside myself," to get souls saved or to reach the heathen with the gospel, if God has always had other ways of accomplishing this task.

Does the writer not know a score of missionary-minded men who would not conceal one least means of winning others? With such frightful and everlasting issues at stake, would these men permit either whim or fancy to determine their choice of instruments to rescue the lost? Would not they seek by the best means, yes, "by all means," to save some? Can such men possibly be more concerned than is God? Beloved reader, we must come to this conclusion: *God is shut up to men to win men.* The master has no other plan. We must accept the responsibility.

(5) If we accept no responsibility for the salvation of others, we may attempt to throw the problem back on a *kind of election that foreordained some souls to be saved and, by the same token, others (those we deny the gospel) to be lost.* In which case (as expanded elsewhere in this

---

1. Unusual angelic proclamations at special seasons (Luke 2), and during the coming tribulation (Rev. 14), when such reinforcements are demanded, need not enter into our present considerations.

book) we might agree with the deacon who rebuked William Carey in his appeal for the spread of the gospel among the heathen: "When God pleases to convert the heathen, he will do it without your help or mine." Evidently the deacon's extreme predestination killed all feeling of missionary obligation. Fortunately Carey's heart of compassion constrained him, in spite of the deacon, to obey Christ's last command to go and seek the lost in India. How dare we, any of us, follow the doctrinal twist (or, better, the downright disobedience) of that deacon and attempt to fall back on the kind of election that would arbitrarily exclude all those unreached souls.

Consider a case in point. A number of our graduates have gone to a field where about 50,000 souls have been converted during the past few years. Are we to conclude that none of those souls would have been finally lost had these young people remained at home in their self-centred lives? Surely these missionaries were God's *means* to this blessed *end*. I hear someone reason: God not only elected those thousands to be saved, but he also decreed the means as well as the end. Yes, it is true that "we are his workmanship, created in Christ Jesus unto good works, which God hath before ordained that we should walk in them" (Eph. 2:10).

What an assurance to us that we may have a God-planned life! It is also true concerning "the lifework which God has planned for us from all eternity" that, as James H. McConkey pointedly tells us, "you may miss it. You may fall short of God's perfect plan for your life." If, my reader, you miss the plan which was to have been God's means of winning those thousands, then you should feel to some degree Paul's "Woe is unto me, if I preach not the gospel." If the means fail, what of the end? Then at whose door shall be laid the failure?

> O church of Christ, what wilt thou say
> When in that awful judgment day
> He charge thee with their doom?
>
> —A. B. Simpson

Shame on the church of Christ that she is forever seeking for an excuse for her disobedience. We readily admit that the unnecessary lostness of many of earth's millions is so paralyzing that only those who intend to be utterly obedient can sympathetically face and embrace the awful responsibility which has been laid at our door. It can scarcely be denied that the chief cause of disobedience to Christ's last command is our utter unwillingness to accept this responsibility and to seek to discharge the debt.

(6) An intimate missionary friend was doing his best to interest a thrifty businessman in the claims of Christ for Africa. After listening to my friend for some time, the businessman bluntly retorted, *"Don't you know that after the church has been translated the Jewish remnant will do a much better job of preaching 'the gospel of the kingdom' than we ever have done?"*

This man had followed to its logical conclusion the teaching that Matthew (including the Great Commission) is for the Jews and that the "Jewish remnant" will do in a few months what we as a church have failed to do in two thousand years. He was unconcerned about the multitudes perishing here and now. He had found an excuse that seemed to relieve him of present missionary responsibility. His lack of conviction regarding Christ's last command arose from an ultra-dispensational handling of the Scriptures, which can furnish Christians with an excuse to nullify the obligations of obedience.

It was the writer's rare privilege to have as one of his personal friends the late Dr. Robert H. Glover, one of the world's great missionary statesmen. In order to confirm the above conclusions regarding the detrimental effect of these teachings of an extreme dispensationalism, we quote from his valuable book, *The Bible Basis of Missions*,[1] a book which should be in the hands of every Christian worker:

> Another view which sadly militates against a united and whole-hearted effort by the true church of Christ to carry out to a finish in this day the evangelization of the world is that advanced by certain gifted teachers of prophecy for whom we have high regard, but with whom we must frankly disagree upon one important point. While holding firmly the truth of the Lord's premillennial coming, they yet relegate to a future

---

1. Published by Bible House of Los Angeles. Reprinted by permission.

company of Jews, subsequent to the rapture of the church, the task of proclaiming the gospel to the whole world, and, accordingly, they relieve the church today of this responsibility....

While some who thus teach are missionary-minded because of their love for the Lord, the natural result upon those who accept this teaching and apply it consistently is to cut the nerve of missionary concern and effort. What the church fails to do in its day will be done by the "Jewish remnant" after the church has been taken away....

We must say that we believe the prodigious achievement attributed to this "Jewish remnant" rests largely upon mere inference, rather than upon any clear and explicit Bible statement, and that by this line of teaching the responsibility which Christ laid upon his church for this age is shifted to others, wrongly and with most unfortunate results.

The Second Coming—and Missions

Before leaving the consideration of how an overdone dispensationalism militates against a whole-hearted enthusiasm for missions, we should observe that the Great Commission is recorded not only in all four Gospels, but also in the first chapter of Acts. Let us briefly observe the first few verses of Acts, in their missionary outlook and dispensational connection. The risen Christ was about to be taken up into heaven, but before his departure he would give his disciples their marching orders. Two angelic beings were nearby, about to announce the return of "this same Jesus," the inference being that while he is away the church will be completing the one and only task left her to accomplish.

Thus missions and the second coming are properly and practically linked the one to the other. Concerning this instance, Dr. Glover says:

The risen Lord comes upon his apostles engaged in what would today be termed a dispensational discussion. They ask him, "Lord, dost thou at this time restore the kingdom to Israel?"—a very natural question for them, as Jews, to ask. But his reply is, "It is not for you to know times or seasons, which the Father hath set within his own authority. But ...." But what? "But ye shall be my witnesses ... unto the uttermost part of the earth."

Can anyone fail to see the point? The Lord brushes aside their discussion about "times and seasons" as irrelevant for the time being, and presses home the thing that was relevant and of vital importance, namely, that they give themselves unreservedly to the one great business and prime objective of the church for the present age, the evangelization of the entire world.

Is this not a word in season to the Lord's people today, and to certain of their leaders in particular, bidding them give less attention to "times and seasons," or, in other words, to profound but largely academic discussions and controversies over various fine points of prophetic interpretation, about which there have always been differences of opinion and always will be, and to devote their time and talents more to the practical aspect of the subject, the carrying out to completion of their risen Lord's last expressed wish and command?

These are wise words from a discerning and Spirit-taught man of God. Yet I have before me as I write a whole volume of sermons delivered at a great congress on prophecy, thirty-three sermons in all, each by some well-known and esteemed prophetic teacher; yet in not one of the many allusions to "end-time" things is there reference to the speeding up of Christ's own missionary program before his return. Concerning such amazing *omissions* in the thinking of great evangelicals, Dr. Glover most graciously expressed only this much of his personal grief:

> We well remember one particular instance when we listened to a masterful address on *The Signs of the Second Coming of Christ*, in which, however, no mention of the missionary sign was made. When we afterward called the speaker's attention to this, sincerely thinking that the omission was purely from lack of time (for the hour was late), he expressed surprise and very frankly said he did not believe missions had anything whatever to do with the return of Christ.
>
> We are by no means disposed to overlook such signs as the steady increase of lawlessness, the rise of political dictatorships, the persecution of the Jews, the growing religious apostasy, and so on. But we would call attention to the fact that these are matters about which, despite our feeling of deep concern, we can do little or nothing, whereas promoting the spread of the gospel to the ends of the earth is something in which all Christians can have an active and effective part.

What Shall We Answer?

Disobedient Christians will be overtaken with awful shame and loss at the judgment of believers when they find themselves excuseless for their past disobedience. Even in this life there comes to the missionary that inevitable and embarrassing moment, that moment of shame and pain, when native Christians begin to question the missionary after the manner of an old Muslim woman in Bengal: "How long is it since Jesus died for sinful people? Look at me; I am old; I have prayed, given alms, gone to the holy shrines, become as dust from fasting, and all this is useless. Where have you been all this time?"

The same cry was echoed from the icy shores of the farthest Northwest Territory. An old Eskimo said to the Bishop of Selkirk, "You have been many moons in this land. Did you know this Good News then? Since you were a boy? and your father knew? Then why did you not come sooner?"

Again, in the snowy heights of the Andes, a Peruvian asked, "How is it that during all the years of my life I have never before heard that Jesus Christ spoke those precious words?"

It was repeated in the white streets of Casablanca, North Africa. Said a Moor to a Bible seller, "Why have you not run everywhere with this Book? Why do so many of my people not know of the Jesus whom it proclaims? Why have you hoarded it to yourselves? Shame on you!"

A missionary in Egypt was telling a woman the story of the love of Jesus, and at the close the woman said, "It is a wonderful story. Do the women in your country believe it?"

"Yes!" said the missionary.

After a moment's reflection came the reply, "I don't think they can believe it, or they would not have been so long in coming to tell us."

A noble pioneer, L. L. Legters, was once preaching the gospel to a group of Latin-American Indians from one of the many totally unevangelized tribes. As he told how the Son of God died on a cross of his own free will that they and all others might escape eternal punishment, one man, who had listened with intense interest, interrupted him, "Señor, when did this one die for us of whom we have never heard? Was it as long as twenty-five years ago?" He stepped back in blank amazement when the answer came, "It was two thousand years ago."

On another occasion, as Mr. Legters was talking to an old Indian chief in South America, the latter asked, "White man, how long since you knew this Jesus way?"

"Chief, it has been a long time."

"How long since your father knew this way?"

"Oh, it was a long time."

"How long since his father knew this way?"

Mr. Legters could only reply, "Oh, it was long ago."

Finally, the old chief, folding his blanket about him, doubtingly concluded, "White man, you wait too long, you wait too long."

The old Indian's reasoning was good. "How do you expect us to believe this news, so good beyond all reckoning, when you have waited 'too long'?"

"So you have come at last," said a Taoist priest as the missionary entered the Chinese temple. The latter had seen the priest listening attentively in the open-air service. The man had long been hungry to know the truth. In some kind of vision he had been impressed that "some day messengers would come from faraway lands." Was it necessary for him to have waited about eighteen long years?

Finally, in *The Growth of a Soul* (published by the China Inland Mission) occurs this reproaching witness against the church: In talking with Hudson Taylor, Mr. Nyi, a Chinese Christian, unexpectedly raised a question, the pain of which was not easily forgotten. "How long have you had the glad tidings in England?" he asked all unsuspectingly.

The young missionary was ashamed to tell him, and vaguely replied that it was several hundred years.

"What," exclaimed Mr. Nyi in astonishment, "several hundreds of years! Is it possible that you have known about Jesus so long, and only now have come to tell us? My father sought the truth for more than twenty years," he continued sadly, "and died without finding it. *Oh, why did you not come sooner?*"

What shall I more say? Time after time from our own conference platform missionaries confess their experiences of pain as their national Christians put the questions: "What about my father? My grandfather? You say God is 'not willing that any should perish,' but *somebody was*. Where were your Christians during all that time?"

The thrust goes home. The missionary cannot make excuses. No doctrinal hideout will help him. He hangs his head; his heart bleeds; his mouth is closed. He can only bear his share of the criminal neglect and bloodguiltiness of those Christians who denied the gospel to the past generations.

Jonah—Runaway Missionary

We cannot close without considering Jonah, that runaway missionary of Old Testament times. Nineveh's judgment lay just ahead of a forty-day *silence*. By this time the disobedient prophet had experienced such mingled miseries and mercies that he had become willing to be recommissioned. Arriving at Nineveh, he cried up and down her streets. By thus warning men of their impending doom, he brought a million souls to repentance.

Then we find this pouting prophet in his little booth outside the city, sitting out those forty days, wondering whether or not God would turn that whole city to a cinder. He was far more concerned over his own comfort, and over the end time of Nineveh, and the fulfilment of prophecy—"yet forty days, and Nineveh shall be overthrown"—than he was over Nineveh's escape from doom. How we abominate the mean, narrow, and bigoted attitude of this man! Yet how he is a photograph of the church today!

True Christians everywhere profess to believe with Jonah that judgment awaits all men outside Christ, that there are cities whose days are numbered, sinners whose cup of iniquity is fast filling, souls whose destiny will soon be sealed. Yet we sit in our little religious booths intensely interested in sermons on prophecy and the ten toes of Daniel's image, whereas a message on missionary endeavor to spare doomed myriads from judgment is monotonous. We do next to nothing to send earth's millions the message that would bring them eternal salvation. We seem unconcerned even to deliver our own souls from bloodguiltiness.

Yet all the while we say we believe that *our silence will seal their fate*—so subtle and hidden can heart unbelief be. We stand rebuked by the words of a gifted and noted unbeliever who said:

> Were I a religionist, did I truly, firmly, *consistently* believe as millions say they do, that the knowledge and the practice of religion in this life influence destiny in another, the spirit of truth be my witness, religion should be to me *everything*. I would cast aside earthly enjoyments as dross, earthly cares as follies, and earthly thoughts and feelings as less than vanity.
>
> Religion should be my first waking thought, and my last image when sleep sinks me into unconsciousness. I would labor in *her* cause alone. I would not labor for the meat that perisheth, nor for the treasure on earth, where moth and rust corrupt, and thieves break through and steal; but only for a crown of glory in heavenly regions, where treasure and happiness are alike beyond the reach of time or chance.
>
> I would take thought for the morrow of eternity alone. I would esteem *one* soul gained to heaven worth a life of suffering. There should be neither worldly prudence nor calculating circumspection in my engrossing zeal. Earthly consequences should never stay my hand nor seal my lips. I would speak to the imagination, awaken the feelings, stir up the passions, arouse the fancy. Earth, its joys and its griefs, should occupy no moments of my thoughts; for these are but the affairs of a portion of eternity so small that no language can express its comparatively infinite littleness.
>
> I would strive to look *but on eternity,* and on the immortal souls around me, soon to be everlastingly miserable or everlastingly happy. I would deem all who thought only of this world, merely seeking to increase temporal happiness, and laboring to obtain temporal goods, pure madmen. I would go forth to the world, and preach to it, in season and out of season; and my text should be, "What shall it profit a man, if he shall gain the whole world and lose his own soul?" (A. S. Ormsby, *Alone with God*).

Letting the World Go By

The mystery is how we can read such words and still sit like Jonah in our little booths, comfortable and content to let earth's Ninevehs—millions without Christ in every land—sink into a lost eternity, yes, sink and be forever lost, not because God did not choose to save them, but because we denied them deliverance. Oh, the crime of it all, this criminal silence! Face it, my reader. What sin can compare with the sin of omission—the criminal silence, the shameful evasion of responsibility, the wicked contentment to let men be swept down into the abyss as though they were only so many autumn leaves!

At the conclusion of a message on Jonah wherein we likened him to the present-day believer, one of our students (now a foreign missionary) wrote the following appropriate lines:

> Jonah built a little booth,
> A shelter from the heat.
> A gourd-vine grew, protection from
> The wind that on him beat.
>
> Jonah rejoiced, exceeding glad
> For this convenient gourd
> Espec'lly since this comfort was
> Provided by the Lord!
>
> "I thank thee, Lord; thou hast been good
> To my dear wife and me;
> We're glad we're in a peaceful land
> Of great prosperity.
>
> "It makes us feel so good—
> This little bungalow—
> The kitchenette, the living room,
> The rug, so soft you know.
>
> "We love our children, ev'ry one;
> We keep them home for God.
> The homeland needs them just as much
> As mission fields abroad.

"And fundamentalists are we,
My children, wife, and I—
So thankful that we're saved by grace,
Secure until we die!

"What didst thou say? Oh—Nineveh?
Well, that's another thing.
Right now we want to praise our God
We're sheltered 'neath his wing!"

Thus fundamental Jonahs to
The Lord their praises tell.
They'll sing, "We're saved and satisfied,"
While Nineveh goes to hell!

—T. Laskowski

The word of warning to ancient Israel rings again in our ears: "Ye have sinned against the Lord; and *be sure your sin will find you out.*"

Turning from all the carnal contentments and excuse-making of this carefree generation of Christians, it is a great relief to bow the shoulder and bear the burden of the Word of the Lord. It is indeed better to be obedient than disobedient. Obedience at its worst, cost what it may, is worlds ahead of an easy-going believism at its best. It is better, yea, very much better, to be burdened and borne down with a great and crushing sense of responsibility for the blood of others than to seek to escape the obligations of an obedient faith. His commandments are not grievous.

Like the dew of the morning, like a drink of cold water, like sunshine after rain, come the words of Hudson Taylor as he battled through and embraced the burden of the Lord on Brighton Beach in 1865:

Unable to bear the sight of a congregation of a thousand or more Christian people rejoicing in their own security while millions were perishing for lack of knowledge, I wandered out on the sands alone, in great spiritual agony. There the Lord conquered my unbelief, and I surrendered myself for this service.

Let me plead with you, my reader, to let no worldliness, no selfishness, no manner of excuse or lie of the Devil stand between you and the complete obedience to the Savior's last command. God warns: "If thou forbear to deliver them that are drawn unto death, and those that are ready to be slain (those slipping to the slaughter—Young); if thou sayest, Behold, we knew it not; doth not he that pondereth the heart consider it? and he that keepeth thy soul, doth not he know it? and shall not he render to every man according to his works?" (Prov. 24:11-12).

Let every reader *go, or let go, or help go.* As much as in us lies, let us rise up and pay our just debt to the last man on earth. Else—how shall we escape SIN FINDING US OUT?

"Who Will Go For Us?"

Are none of us bound to go? Does the divine voice appeal to our thousands of preachers and find no response, so that again it cries, "Whom shall I send?" Here and there a young man, perhaps with little qualification and no experience, offers himself, and he may or may not be welcomed. But can it be true that the majority of educated, intelligent, Christian young men are more willing to let the heathen be damned than to let the treasures of the world go into other hands?

We shall not always throw the emphasis on the last word, "me," but read it also thus, "Here am I, *send* me." He is willing to go, but he does not want to go without being sent, and so the prayer is, "Lord, *send* me. I beseech thee of thine infinite grace qualify me, open the door for me, and direct my way. I do not need to be forced, but I would be commissioned. I do not ask for compulsion, but I do ask for guidance. I would not run of my own head, under the notion that I am doing God service. *Send* me, then, O Lord, if I may go; guide me, instruct me, prepare me, and strengthen me."

I feel certain that some of you are eager to go for my Lord and Master wherever he appoints. Keep not back, I pray you. Brother, make no terms with God. Put it, "Here am I; send me—where thou wilt, to the wildest region, or even to the jaws of death: I am thy soldier; put me in the front of the battle if thou wilt, or bid me lie in the trenches; give me gallantly to charge at the head of my regiment, or give me silently to sap and mine the foundations of the enemy's fortresses. Use me as thou wilt; *send* me, and I will go. I leave all else to thee; only here I am, thy willing servant, wholly consecrated to thee."

—Rev. Charles H. Spurgeon

8

Occupy Till I Come

For the Son of Man is come to seek and to save that which was lost.

And as they heard these things, he added and spake a parable, because he was nigh to Jerusalem, and because they thought that the kingdom of God should immediately appear.

He said therefore, A certain nobleman went into a far country to receive for himself a kingdom, and to return.

And he called his ten servants, and delivered them ten pounds, and said unto them, Occupy till I come.

But his citizens hated him, and sent a message after him, saying, We will not have this man to reign over us.

And it came to pass, that when he was returned, having received the kingdom, then he commanded these servants to be called unto him, to whom he had given the money, that he might know how much every man had gained by trading.

Then came the first, saying, Lord, thy pound hath gained ten pounds.

And he said unto him, Well, thou good servant: because thou hast been faithful in a very little, have thou authority over ten cities.

And the second came, saying, Lord, thy pound hath gained five pounds.

And he said likewise to him, Be thou also over five cities. And another came, saying, Lord, behold, here is thy pound, which I have kept laid up in a napkin:

For I feared thee, because thou art an austere man: thou takest up that thou layedst not down, and reapest that thou didst not sow.

And he saith unto him, Out of thine own mouth will I judge thee, thou wicked servant. Thou knewest that I was an austere man, taking up that I laid not down, and reaping that I did not sow:

Wherefore then gavest not thou my money into the bank, that at my coming I might have required mine own with usury?

And he said unto them that stood by, Take from him the pound, and give it to him that hath ten pounds.

(And they said unto him, Lord, he hath ten pounds.)

For I say unto you, That unto every one which hath shall be given; and from

89

him that hath not, even that he hath shall be taken away from him.
But those mine enemies, which would not that I should reign over them, bring
hither, and slay them before me.

Luke 19:10–27

The King is coming. That is a great certainty. But Jesus gave the parable of the pounds to correct the countrywide expectation that the Messianic kingdom would be presently set up as soon as he entered Jerusalem. Christ did not contradict the idea of the literal kingdom. He only corrected the notion of its "immediately appearing."

"He said, therefore, A certain nobleman went into a far country to receive for himself a kingdom, and to return" (Luke 19:12). If any man in a remote province of the Roman Empire aspired to become ruler of that realm, he must journey in person to Rome and obtain directly from the hands of the reigning Caesar the title and commission to rule. Under this figure Christ teaches the necessity, as well as the meaning, of his own early departure from earth to heaven, there to receive the kingdom from the ruler of the universe. But he teaches his return also, without which the object of his going away would remain unfulfilled. He is going to return—to rule.

Occupy Till I Come

"And he called his ten servants, and delivered them ten pounds, and said unto them, Occupy till I come" (19:13). Upon leaving this world the Lord Jesus left his full earthly interests and resources in the charge of the entire body of his "servants"—all to be employed until his return.

While our "nobleman," our absent but coming King, is away, we are to remember that our gospel program (for it is not a *kingdom* that is left to our charge) is but a business, an estate, a commission. And what are the confines of this estate or the territorial limits of this business enterprise? Our God is the Lord of all the earth. Did God so love the world? Then "Go ye into all the world, and preach the gospel to every creature" (Mark 16:15). The bounds of responsibility must include the entire world, every tongue and tribe and nation. And not merely are we to touch each tribe with a single testimony; we are bidden to reach all men during each successive generation of the entire dispensation.

"With this worldwide program before us, the church is never to talk of 'home work' until she has found her home in all the world. Home work is worldwide work, on the simple principle of equality" (Stevens). Let us then "occupy" as much territory as ever we can "till he comes."

1. The Pounds

This question is in order: What is the meaning of the pound in this parable? It is to be noted that there is nothing here of earthly or human resources. The "pounds" must mean the heavenly resources that Jesus used and left to us that we might "occupy" for him in his absence. Very significant is the expression in Luke 19:16: "Lord, thy pound hath gained ten pounds." It is the Lord's own pound. It is the same for each servant. And he gives the pound its productive power. It is the gospel pound, "the power of God unto salvation."

The object in view determines the means to be employed. Christ himself stated it in the first verse we quoted: "For the Son of Man is come to seek and to save that which was lost" (Luke 19:10). He had just occupied some "lost" territory in the heart of Zacchaeus. On that background He spoke this parable.

It is not difficult to see some five aspects of gospel agency which Christ still loves to use and to energize, in order that the lost may be sought and found.

Let us then break up this "pound" into five aspects of gospel resource:

2. Gospel Words

We are commanded to "preach the word" (2 Tim. 4:2). The gospel is the good seed we are to sow everywhere. "The field is the world." Ours is the "word of reconciliation." And this gospel preaching need never change with the times, or with the fashion of the day. It does not have to be brought "up to date," for ever since the fall of man it has never been out of date. Genesis 3 is most historic and is ever up to date.

We need to beware of updating our message to suit modern thinking. The early preachers borrowed nothing religious from the world around them. Nor do we need to borrow from the earth. Why go down to Egypt for help? The purpose of the preached word at the beginning was the saving of the lost to the uttermost. It has no other purpose now.

How necessary are these gospel words! Let the following account show us how desperately they are needed:

> Two African chiefs once came to Dr. Chalmers and said, "We want Christian teachers; will you send them?" Chalmers had no one to send, and told them so. Two years passed, and those two chiefs came again. Dr. Chalmers himself happened to be at liberty, and went. To his surprise, he saw the whole village on their knees in perfect silence. He asked one of the chiefs what they were doing, and received the reply, "Praying."
>
> "But you are not saying anything," said Dr. Chalmers. "White man," the chief answered, "we do not know what to *say*. For two years, every Sunday morning, we have met here; and for four hours we have been on our knees, and we have been praying like that, but we do not know what to say."
>
> What a picture of waiting nations!—waiting for the gospel message!

How precious this gospel message should be to us! "A banker of Edinburgh said to D. M. Panton: "Come here, and I will show you the greatest treasure I possess." And he brought forth a singed Bible—thrown out of the fire by one of his martyred relatives. He said, "This is the price of my freedom."

What a harvest of martyrs our gospel message has made! These life-giving words have quickened souls in every country, in every culture, in every clime. Consider how this blessed Bible—blood-soaked, battle-scarred, fire-singed, tattered and torn by the critics—think how this book has come forth from the critics' den unbitten by the lions of liberalism and unsinged by the fires of falsehood.

Finally a word of warning. Remember the "wicked servant" who buried his pound in a napkin. Let not the reader wrap up the gospel word in the neat napkin of a lovely leather-bound Bible, nor in concealed gospel tracts, nor yet in a muzzled testimony.

3. Gospel Works

Our gospel must be lived out—in word and *deed.* Our testimonies must be consistent, by *life* as well as by *lip.* The order is: Plant your feet of open-mouthed testimony, then live the life that all men may see, not your good words, but your "good works," and glorify God.

A Muslim was an honest man. After his wife had heard a missionary, he said, "Is it a true Word—this of a Savior who loves us and can save us from our sins?" So he read the New Testament, but he could not believe it to be true "because he had never seen the life lived that was spoken of in that book." He later saw that kind of life lived out in some of his fellow-nationals—and himself believed.

It has been well said that the only Bible men of the world read is one about six feet tall and bound in human skin. Professing Christians must also be possessing Christians. A little lassie asked her mother a pertinent question: "Where do the church people put all the joy they were singing about in church?" People may seldom read their Bibles, but they are reading us Christians.

> You are writing a gospel
> A chapter each day,
> By the deeds that you do,
> And the words that you say.
> Men read what you write,
> Whether faithless or true;
> Say, what is the gospel
> According to you?

Our gospel words must be backed up by good *works.* Here is how a true gospel herald preached the Good News to the heathen "down under."

> A missionary in New Guinea returned to his home after several years of service.
> His friend said to him, "Jones, tell me what you found at your station in New Guinea."

"Found! I found something that looked more hopeless than if I had been sent into the jungle to a lot of tigers."

"What do you mean?"

"Why, those people were so degraded that they seemed utterly devoid of moral sense. They were worse than beasts. If a mother were carrying her little baby, and the baby began to cry, she would throw it into the ditch and let it die. If a man saw his father break his leg, he would leave him upon the roadside to die. They had no compassion whatever. They did not know what it meant."

"Well, what did you do for people like that? Did you preach to them?"

"Preach? No! I lived."

"Lived? How did you live?"

"When I saw a baby crying, I picked it up and comforted it. When I saw a man with a broken leg, I mended it. When I saw people in distress, I took them in and pitied them. I took care of them. I lived that way. And those people began to come to me and say, 'What does this mean? What are you doing this for?' Then I had my chance and I preached the gospel."

"Did you succeed?"

"When I left, I left a church!"

—*Sunday School Times*

A great preacher closed his sermon with an earnest and eloquent gospel appeal. Among the score or more who responded was a woman of wealth and social distinction. She asked permission to speak a few words to the audience.

"I want you to know," she said, "just why I came forward tonight. It was not because of any word spoken by the preacher. I stand here because of the influence of a little woman who sits before me. Her fingers are rough with toil; the hard work of many years has stooped her low; she is just a poor, obscure washerwoman who has served in my home for many years. I have never known her to become impatient, speak an unkind word, or do a dishonorable deed. I know of countless little acts of unselfish love that adorn her life.

"Shamefacedly, let me say that I have openly sneered at her faith, and laughed at her fidelity to God. Yet, when my little girl was taken away, it was this woman who caused me to look beyond the grave and shed my first tear of hope. The sweet magnetism of her life has led me to Christ. I covet the thing that has made her life so beautiful."

At the request of the minister, the little woman was led forward, her eyes streaming with glad tears, and such a shining face as one seldom sees on this earth. "Let me introduce you," said he, "to the real preacher of the evening," and the great audience arose in silent, though not tearless, respect.

—The Gospel Herald

4. Gospel Power

When the apostle writes his first letter to the Thessalonians, he reminds those converts: "Our gospel came not unto you in word only, but also in power, and in the Holy Ghost, and in much assurance" (1 Thess. 1:5). Much gospel is given out "in word only," a gospel unaccompanied by power, a gospel not "in the Holy Ghost, and not in much assurance." It is even possible to practise an unspiritual Christianity, "having a form of godliness, but denying the power thereof" (2 Tim. 3:5).

Without this accompanying power the glorious gospel is in word only, in "the letter that killeth." Somebody has said that if the Holy Ghost were taken out of the world the church could carry on as usual and would not miss him for years. Shame on us! Does the flesh then have such dominion today that we would not even miss the presence and power of the Spirit? A bold and godly professor once said to his class: "Gentlemen, remember that without the illumination of the Spirit, theology is not only a cold stone, it is a deadly poison."

Dr. Jonathan Goforth had been a missionary in China for years without witnessing the "greater works" that Jesus promised with the coming of the Spirit. Through a period of intensive preparation, he came to experience the Spirit's convicting and converting power.

The final crisis came in the midst of an evening prayer service that was dull and dry as dust. "There had not been seen a tear on a Chinaman's cheek," he said, "for some twenty years."

In the midst of that service the Lord rebuked him: "You hypocrite, you do not love so-and-so the way you should."

Dr. Goforth held out and limited the Holy Ghost for some time. But he finally yielded and the Spirit took over. Tears and prayers were mingled until eleven o'clock.

While the missionary resisted and blocked the Spirit, the "power" of the gospel was untapped and unused—was not allowed to work. Rather, that gospel resource was "buried" in the fleshly self-life of an unyielded servant. And the result? Chinese hearts—unfilled territories, unplowed lands, uncultivated acres—were unoccupied for Christ, all because of an unanointed missionary.

5. Gospel Prayers

Christ's active ministry consisted of words and works. Paul sought "to make the Gentiles obedient, by word and deed" (Rom. 15:18). But behind both Christ and Paul was a prayer ministry. Peter said: "It is not fit that we should forsake the word of God, and serve tables …. We will continue steadfastly in prayer, and in the ministry of the word" (Acts 6:2, 4 ASV). Peter gave top priority to prevailing prayer.

How easy to have a formal prayer, or a routine bit of prayer, instead of praying through every problem beforehand. A great Bible expositor is reported to have said recently on his deathbed: "I have written too much and prayed too little." We need to take heed to Samuel's word on Israel's behalf: "God forbid that I should sin against the Lord in ceasing to pray for you" (1 Sam. 12:23). The greatest sins of the saints are sins of *omission* rather than *commission*. And the first and greatest omission is doubtless that of prayer.

The greatest work is knee work. J. O. Fraser of the China Inland Mission (now the Overseas Missionary Fellowship) wrote to his mother:

> Christians at home can do as much for foreign missions as those actually on the field. I believe it will be known only on the last day how much has been accomplished in missionary work by the prayers of earnest believers at home. Such work does not consist in curio exhibitions, lantern lectures, interesting reports, and so on. Good as they may be, these are only the fringe, not the root of the matter. Solid, lasting missionary work is done on our knees.

—Behind the Ranges[1]

---

1. From *Behind the Ranges* by Taylor, Copyright 1975. Moody Press. Moody Bible Institute of Chicago. Used by permission.

Have we kept this prayer ministry buried under a carnal flesh life? We cannot *live* in the flesh and *pray* in the Spirit. Only by a revival of spiritual life can we experience a renewal of the prayer life. A failing prayer life must issue from a faulty spiritual life.

If it be true that "ye have not because ye ask not," let us not succumb to the sin of prayerlessness. Prayer must come to take precedence over all other public ministry.

I recall a praying woman on her deathbed in California. As a missionary-minded prayer warrior she noticed as she studied the missionary needs in a particular part of Africa that there was a certain territory that had not one missionary.

Furthermore, as she read her Bible, she found that when King Hezekiah was sick unto death God added fifteen years to his life. This woman, therefore, prayed: "Lord, if you will add fifteen years to my life, I will pray missionaries into that unoccupied territory of Africa." And that woman lived to see that field occupied for Christ by missionaries that she had prayed out. And a missionary society in an adjacent territory recognized that particular area as the mission field of this praying invalid. Thus this intercessor occupied for Christ by putting the prayer pound to work.

6. Gospel Suffering

Did Christ learn obedience by the things he suffered? And did he become the author of salvation to those who obey and follow him? All who will live godly in Christ Jesus must suffer persecution. Manifold will be our temptations and trials for righteousness' sake.

If we are Christ's followers, we must become his fellow-sufferers. It is given us on behalf of Christ not only to believe on him, but also "to suffer for his sake" (Phil. 1:29). We are to take up our cross "daily." While we are not to think of sharing in Christ's atoning sacrifice on his cross, we cannot overlook our partaking with him in a sacrificial spirit for the sake of others. Listen to Paul: "Who now rejoice in my sufferings for you, and fill up that which is behind of the afflictions of Christ in my flesh for his body's sake, which is the church, whereof I am made a minister" (Col. 1:24-25).

Paul insistently urged upon Timothy: "Be thou partaker of the afflictions of the gospel" (2 Tim. 1:8), or, as Bishop Moule puts it, "Suffer with the suffering gospel." Afflictions and suffering are native to the gospel. "In putting your gospel pound to work, Timothy, do not shrink from adding this essential ingredient."

It is where we embrace our cross in suffering and sacrifice that Christ comes to be seen. Many a hard-hearted heathen has had his heart broken by witnessing the ability of his fellow-nationals to suffer for Christ's sake. We thus prove ourselves to be "heirs of God, and joint-heirs with Christ; if so be that we suffer with him, that we may be also glorified together" (Rom. 8:17). Anyone who wills to occupy till Christ returns dare not cringe from the cup of suffering, but must take it up cheerfully and drink it brimful.

What strangers we are to talk about gospel sufferings "in the land of peace"! Can we not make the matter practical? Let us listen to a little sufferer and learn a lesson on how to be a missionary:

> "I am not anxious to die easy, when he died hard!" So said, not long ago, in a London attic, lying crippled and comfortless, a little disciple of the Man of Sorrows. He had "seen the Lord," in a strangely unlikely conversion, and had found a way of serving him; it was to drop written fragments of his Word from the window onto the pavement below. And for this silent mission he would have no liberty if he were moved, in his last weeks, to a comfortable "Home."
>
> So he would rather serve his beloved Redeemer thus, "pleasing not himself," than be soothed in body, and gladdened by surrounding kindness, but with less "fellowship of his sufferings." Illustrious confessor—sure to be remembered when "the Lord of the servants cometh"!
>
> —Bishop Moule in *The Epistle to the Romans*

"Occupy till I come." With these mighty gospel resources what hinders the fulfilment of this great commission? Where is the blockade? Let a notable missionary statesman answer that question:

> A prominent missionary statesman of the past generation set forth the kind of revival that would affect the vitality of the church and determine the eternal welfare of untold millions:

"The occupation of the unoccupied fields is the distinctive and crowning challenge of this missionary age …. And what is the price of their occupation? The pathway which leads to their occupation lies across other unoccupied fields—great areas these—in our own lives and hearts, not yet surrendered to the will of Christ, not yet fully occupied by his Spirit, not yet touched by the flame of a perfect love and consecration. Only as he is permitted to fully occupy these nearer areas in our own lives will he be able to gain entrance into those more distant fields of the unoccupied world."

—Charles Watson in *Progress of World-Wide Missions*
by Dr. Robert Glover

The King is coming. And the day of reckoning. As his servants, are we putting his pound to work? Or is there still some unoccupied territory in the reader's life calling for Christ's incoming and occupation?

Missions

William Adams Brown, whose name is almost synonymous with "foreign missions," used to silence all thinking objectors in his audiences with this striking apologetic:

(1) Every book in the New Testament was written by a foreign missionary.

(2) Every letter in the New Testament that was written to an individual was written to a convert of a foreign missionary.

(3) Every epistle in the New Testament that was written to a church was written to a foreign-missionary church.

(4) The disciples were called Christian first in a foreign-missionary community.

(5) Of the twelve apostles chosen by Jesus, every apostle except one became a missionary.

(6) The only one among the twelve apostles who did not become a missionary became a traitor.

(7) The problems which arose in the early Church were largely questions of missionary procedure.

(8) According to the apostles, missionary service is the highest expression of Christian life.

—Selected

9

Missionary Stakes

Sing, O barren, thou that didst not bear; break forth into singing, and cry aloud, thou that didst not travail with child: for more are the children of the desolate than the children of the married wife, saith the Lord.

Enlarge the place of thy tent, and let them stretch forth the curtains of thine habitations: spare not, lengthen thy cords, and strengthen thy stakes.

(Isaiah 54:1-2)

Isaiah bids the Israelites as the restored wife of the Lord: "Enlarge the place of thy tent ... spare not, lengthen thy cords, and *strengthen thy stakes;* for thou shalt break forth on the right hand and on the left; and thy seed shall inherit the Gentiles" (Isa. 54:2-3).[1] Repentant and restored Israelites will yet be so many that their "tent" will have to be enlarged by lengthening the cords. But this will make it necessary that the *stakes* supporting the tent be strengthened. Those who have camped or lived in tents will understand this figure and the necessity.

William Carey found in this portion a great appeal for missionary vision and outreach. However, when he insisted on "the duty of Christians to attempt the spread of the gospel among heathen nations," he met with the most stubborn opposition from the assembly of believers. The doctrinally warped moderator vehemently rebuked Mr. Carey: "Young man, sit down. You are a miserable enthusiast. When God pleases to convert the heathen, he will do it without your aid or mine."

Thus young Carey found doctrinal and practical difficulty strengthening the stakes of missionary conviction in his home church before

---

1. This compilation of missionary sermons should include the writer's message, "Seven Stakes to Be Driven," which appears in *Prairie Pillars* (pages 59–72). We therefore publish that message here in a slightly altered and abbreviated form.

the expanding vision of his missionary tent could be supported and enlarged. That strengthening of missionary obligation and responsibility is again sorely needed if God's people are to be enlarged in heart to fulfil the Great Commission. There are some stakes of deep conviction that must be driven in on the home front, or we shall experience little or no missionary expansion abroad.

1. The Authority of the Scriptures Regarding the Lostness of the Lost

Why is it that God's people, even his true evangelical people, are losing their conviction about the lost condition of the heathen? Does not some of the fault lie in our questioning the absolute and final authority of the Scriptures? All the great missionary leaders of the past and the present would agree with J. Hudson Taylor, the founder of the China Inland Mission (now the Overseas Missionary Fellowship), who declared near the end of his life that he would never have thought of going to China had he not been convinced that the Chinese were lost, and that they needed Christ in order to be saved.

Nearly forty years ago a church leader made a clear-cut confession in explanation of the retrenchment of missions. He said that God's people are "no longer gripped by a moving conviction that men without Christ are eternally lost." Let us be frankly honest. When you and I see men, men of culture and refinement, men with all the amenity and touch of Western civilization, is it not difficult to believe in the infinite lostness of these lost ones? So easily we fall into the lethargy of a false mercy and an indulgent kindness. We begin to reason within ourselves, "Can such good citizens, whether the heathen at home or abroad, be as lost as I have been led to believe?"

We must come back to the authority and plain teaching of Scripture. Let every honest Christian consider the state of the heathen as set forth in such Scriptures as the following, and he can no longer doubt the lostness of the lost: Psa. 9:17; 97:7; 135:15–18; Acts 26:18; Rom. 1:18–20; 2:8-9; 2:12–15; 3:10–23; 1 Cor. 9:16; 10:20; 2 Cor. 5:17; Eph. 2:1–3, 12; 4:17–19; 1 Thess. 4:5; 2 Thess. 1:8-9; Jude 7, 14, 15; Rev. 20:12–15; 21:8.

Let us ponder these passages prayerfully until we are gripped with the conviction that men anywhere and everywhere without Christ are lost and doomed unto eternal death unless they be saved. If these things be not so then John 3:16 is a meaningless hoax.

2. Christ, the Only Savior

Was it for this already lost world that God gave his beloved Son as the one and only Savior from sin? Did I need Christ to be saved? Could Christ alone meet my need? What alone could wash away my sin? Is Christ for me the only way, the only truth, the only life (John 14:6)? Candidly, could I come to God through any other? For me as a Bible believer these questions have only one answer.

No less do the heathen need the same Savior, the same precious blood for their cleansing. They likewise are in the same desperate need of the "One (and only) mediator between God and men, the man Christ Jesus" (1 Tim. 2:5). Concerning all sinners there is no distinction, "for all have sinned, and fall short of the glory of God" (Rom. 3:23 ASV). Where is there a "mouth" on either side of the ocean that needs *not* to "be stopped"? Where is any heathen that is not to take his place as one of a "world guilty before God"? (Rom. 3:19).

Let those who dream that God has other ways of saving lost men, whether at home or abroad—let them trace up their controversy to its logical conclusion. Where must they finally and inevitably come? They must conclude that the All-Wise blundered in sending his only begotten Son to redeem men who, although without God and without Christ, were not completely without hope.

And must such disputants further charge Christ with the unparalleled folly of leaving heaven to die for persons not hopelessly lost, those not altogether cursed, and to expire under a sense of Heaven's wrath to save from hell people who were in no least danger of ever going there? Was the same Savior ignorant or mistaken in commanding his disciples to go into all the world and preach the gospel as the only saving message to redeem guilty men? To question whether Christ is the one and only way of rescue for the heathen is to question the necessity of Christ for my personal salvation.

Let us make no truce with the father of lies. We dare not think "above that which is written (1 Cor. 4:6). If we take the Scriptures at face value in their plain self-evident meaning, we can come to only one conclusion, viz., that apart from Christ men are without God in this world and without hope for the next. "There is none other name under heaven given among men, whereby we must be saved" (Acts 4:12).

Not only is there no other name whereby we must be saved, but it is by Christ that God will judge all men. See Matt. 25:31-32; John 3:14–19; Acts 17:31; Rom. 1:16–20; 2:16; 2 Thess. 1:8; Rev. 20:12–15.

3. A Deepened Spiritual Life

A great Bible teacher of the past generation was originally an opposer to the truth of the second coming of Christ. But one night he faced the demand for full consecration. The next morning he thought, "I'd love to see the Lord come again." He forthwith loved "his appearing," not because he had been argued into the truth, but because of his deepened spiritual life. "The Spirit and the bride say, Come." Likewise the Spirit-filled life prepares the heart for fresh obedience to Christ.

Would we lengthen the cords of the missionary tent? We must strengthen the stake of the consecrated life. We must go deeper *within* if we would go farther *abroad*. Missions is essentially the work and overflow of the Spirit. "The Spirit of Christ is the very spirit of missions" (A. T. Pierson). Church history abounds with instances of fresh effusions of the Spirit that preceded and gave birth to new missionary obedience and outreach.

The great commission was inseparably linked with the coming and working of the Holy Spirit. "Pentecost was the essential preparation for missions, and missions was the logical and inevitable result of Pentecost" (Dr. Robert Glover). Christ's promise to the first disciples still stands: "Ye shall receive power, after that the Holy Ghost is come upon you: and ye shall be witnesses unto me both in Jerusalem, and in all Judaea, and in Samaria, and unto the uttermost part of the earth" (Acts 1:8).

We might add that no amount of missionary information or argument can create a missionary-minded Christian if there remains any lingering argument with the Spirit of God. In his proclamation of Christ and in the face of an embargo on his speech Peter declared: "We are his witnesses of these things; and so is also the Holy Ghost, whom God hath given to them that obey him" (Acts 5:32).

4. The Explicit Command of Christ

An English clergyman once asked some British soldiers, "If Queen Victoria were to issue a proclamation and, placing it in the hands of her army and navy, were to say, 'Go ye into all the world and proclaim it to every creature,' how long do you think it would take to do it?"

One of those brave fellows, accustomed to obeying orders without hesitation or delay, and at the peril of life, promptly answered, "Well, I think we could manage it in about eighteen months."

"This command (Mark 16:15) seems to me to be strictly a missionary injunction, and, as far as I can see, those to whom it was first delivered regarded it in that light; so that, apart altogether from lower reasons, my going forth is a matter of obedience to a plain command; and in place of seeking to *assign* a reason for *going* abroad, I would prefer to say that I have failed to discover any reason why I should stay at home."

—James Gilmour of Mongolia

The cause of missions needs no other justification, no other argument, no other plea, than the plain, explicit command of Christ. He is sovereign Commander-in-Chief of the campaign. He offered us neither advice nor suggestion when he gave us his orders: "As my Father hath sent me, even so send I you" (John 20:21). That was a declaration of his will, his purpose, his plan.

With "all authority in heaven and in earth," he commissions us, yea, commands us, to "Go." And when he said "Go," he did not say "Stay." Nor did he hint that his disciples wait for a call, or a special voice. A *verse* is better than a *voice*. If we have an ear to hear, the voice is back of the verse.

We hear much today about challenge, the challenge of missions. It seems to mean that we should mount up to the occasion, should measure up to the opportunity, should heroically respond to so great and good a cause. All very well. Truly no higher challenge is conceivable. No nobler achievement can be imagined.

However, achievement can be an appeal to our nobility, our manhood, our valor, our instinct for conquest. We fear there has been too much challenge to conquest instead of obedience to command. Our commission is "for obedience to the faith among all nations" (Rom. 1:5; 15:18, 16:26). This obedience must begin with ourselves, by personal capitulation to the Lordship of Christ, by obedience to his last command. Our captain still says: "If ye love me, ye will keep my commandments" (John 14:15 ASV).

The Roman centurion (Luke 7:1–10) understood what it meant to be under command. This man came to Jesus on behalf of his sick slave. Hear his request: "Say in a word, and my servant shall be healed." Why did he say that? It was a great expression of faith. Listen to his reasoning: "I *also* am a man set under authority." Note that wee word *"also."* Why did he say that? There was a close connection between his own order of life and that of the Lord Jesus. He did not say, as we might have expected, "I am a man *in* authority." Nor did he say, "I am a man *under* authority," but he said, "I *also* am a man set under authority." What did he mean?

He revealed that as he himself lived in complete submission to higher authority, so the Lord Jesus lived under complete authority to Heaven. He saw that Jesus possessed authority over diseases, as complete as his own authority over his soldiers, or as Caesar's authority over himself. "For I also am a man set under authority, having under me soldiers, and I say unto one, Go, and he goeth; and to another, Come, and he cometh; and to my servant, Do this, and he doeth it" (Luke 7:8). When the centurion uttered his orders, those soldiers heard the roar of Rome. They responded right now. Explicit were their orders! Implicit was their obedience.

Now this man believes that Christ's word of command—a word with ultimate and final authority regardless of distance—is sufficient to send sickness away. Is Jesus an almighty Master and King vested with all authority? Then diseases, like obedient servants, must at once depart when he bids them go.

What was the secret of this man's "so great faith"? He simply saw that Jesus was *under* authority, and was therefore *in* authority. His obedient faith was based upon Jesus being so under the authority of God that he was completely in authority over all the things of life, whether they be disease or distance or difficulty. He could therefore say to disease, "Go," and it goeth.

Is Christ's word of command—if he be Lord at all, so Lord over all—is that word so explicit and sufficient to send not only diseases, but his own disciples to the ends of the earth? He still commands his obedient servants the way he commissioned Saul of Tarsus: "He said unto me, *Depart: for I will send thee far hence unto the Gentiles*" (Acts 22:21). Years later the great apostle could say, "I was not disobedient unto the heavenly vision" (Acts 26:19).

Let the stake of loving obedience to our sovereign Lord be driven deeply into our sluggish affections! Might we have more men for foreign missions if we made our motto that of the French Foreign Legion:

> If I falter, push me on;
> If I stumble, pick me up;
> If I retreat, shoot me.

5. Conviction Regarding God's Program of Missions

As Christian leaders we are at fault in having presumed that our congregations, yes, our Christian folk, old and young, are familiar with the fact of missions. Many Christians will agree that missions are good, are noble, are necessary, but comparatively few of these same Christians are vitally involved in God's program of missions. The responsibility and burden of missions must be pressed alike upon parents and their children. Many parents, and some pastors, say:

"Yes, we believe that some of our young ones may go as missionaries, but we do not press the matter or agitate the question among them." Where are the young men? The mission field needs men. God is saying, "Look ye out from among you … men." Our churches should be seeking out and sending the finest of our young men. Think of a minister of an important district confessing that no young man has ever gone as a missionary from his congregation. And there are scores of parishes whose history is sadly similar.

A godly clergyman once said, "There was nothing to prevent my having gone out as a missionary when I was a young man; I had no home ties. I could easily have gone. But *nobody suggested it to* me!" Just so, there are men of the right sort who would go if it were "suggested to them," if only we "agitated the question among them."

How can we be so blissfully content to see only the occasional one of our number become a missionary? Rather, let us embrace the grand motto: "Every Christian a missionary." No, not all in the actual going abroad, but each one, whether at home or abroad, equally informed, equally dedicated, equally sacrificial, equally ready to go or stay, as God guides. And the net result? Many more of our young people will go to the more needy "regions beyond."

What is God's program for this age? Let us not be deluded into dreaming of a gospel program whereby society will be reformed, politics will be purged, nations will be Christianized, social and moral evils will be overthrown, and the millennial reign of peace will be realized. Most of us have not been sidetracked into such an unscriptural utopian dream of bliss. Far be it! But the gospel imperative for us is to be fired with a passion for God's unchanged mandate of missions, not as one of the conversion of the world, but as one of worldwide witness—winning the lost.

"The task enjoined is seen to be, not that of bringing the whole world to Christ, but of bringing Christ to the whole world; not converting all nations as such, but calling out of all nations a people for his name, who shall constitute the true church or bride of Christ" (Glover). The world is indeed a sinking ship, and it is our supreme task to get as many into the lifeboat as possible—as soon as possible. It is now or never for these.

Such is the simplicity of God's missionary program. This unfinished task of evangelism is the first and foremost business of the church. Nor do we need a "social gospel," so-called, of greater breadth that will include in its scope the industrial, civic, economic, and political life of the people. We can leave the government of the world till Christ comes. When the King returns, "having received the kingdom," not from our hands but from the Most High, he will institute the reign of the necessary "rod of iron." The government will then be "upon his shoulder."

It is for us to leave the civilizing and Christianizing of society to be the incidental side effects or by-products of the presence of the gospel of Christ. Let us give our time, our strength, our effort, our money, our days to the supreme and superhuman task of making Christ known "to every creature" (Mark 16:15).

Some thirty years ago a great church leader made this clear-cut confession regarding the retrenchment of missions:

> Why is it that the interest in foreign missions is everywhere lagging and that gifts are falling off? It is because the Christian people are no longer gripped by a burning conviction that men everywhere are lost without Christ. The sense of urgency, immediate danger, of a crisis in salvation has largely disappeared. Many of our preachers no longer preach as dying men to dying men. Our forefathers believed that men everywhere without Christ were in imminent danger of facing the wrath of God.
>
> Our modern world has largely lost this urgent note in salvation. We need to restore it. It is this loss of a mighty conviction about salvation and of both a present and future disaster to the soul and to modern civilization without Christianity that has cut the nerve of missionary obligation and enthusiasm.

—Prairie Pillars, Page 67

6. The Passion of Sacrificial Devotion to Christ

David Livingstone, great pioneer and living sacrifice for Africa, said: "God had only one Son, and he was a missionary." God so loved that he gave. By love compelled—that must be our motivation. Only love's sweet compulsion can carry us through. When the going gets tough, the tough get going—and keep going. But only those motivated by a deep, unfailing love can bear all things, believe all things, hope all things, endure all things. Only such can say, "The love of Christ constraineth us."

There will always be missionary risks, as well as difficulties, that will test our heart's devotion. While the hazards of missionary life are not what they once were, there will always be risks, many where the gospel has never gone. The missionary must still face hostile mobs. Long-neglected fields will still yield their martyrs. Many have thus already lost their lives. Many more have lost their lives from disease, for they work often in unhealthy climates. The people among whom they labor are subject to terrible diseases and death-dealing plagues.

But by love constrained they do not falter. When Alexander Mackay was being sent out to Africa, he said at the farewell meeting: "I want to remind the committee that within six months they will hear that one of this party of eight missionaries will be dead. When the news comes, do not be cast down, but send someone else immediately to take the vacant place." Such is the passionate devotion to Christ that marks the true missionary.

> Oh, by thy cross and passion, Lord,
> Grant us this plea, this sovereign plea,
> Save us from choosing peace for sword,
> And give us souls to give to thee.
>
> —Amy Carmichael

What better emblem can Christ's disciples have than that of the Baptist Missionary Society, an ox standing midway between the plow and the altar, and underneath the words, "Ready for either or both"—ready for sacrifice or ready for service, as God may choose. This stake of sacrificial devotion to Christ himself must be driven deeply into our *sagging* discipleship.

Consider the "weaker vessel" and woman-evangelist, Mrs. Booth-Clibborn, better known as the Marechale of France. How could she ever hope to conquer in religion-ridden and infidel France! Listen to the testimony of that frail little woman:

When I went to France, I said to Christ: "I in you and you in me!" And many a time in confronting single-handed a laughing, scoffing crowd, I have said, "You and I are enough for them. I won't fail you, and you won't fail me." That is something of which we have only touched the fringe. That is a truth almost hermetically sealed. It would be sacrilege, it would be desecration, it would be wrong, unfair, unjust if divine power were given on any other terms than absolute self-abandonment.

When I went to France, I said to Jesus, "I will suffer anything if you will give me the keys." And if I am asked what was the secret of our power in France, I answer: First, love; second, love; third, love. And if you ask how to get it, I answer: First, by sacrifice; second, by sacrifice; third, by sacrifice. Christ loved us passionately, and loves to be loved passionately.

—From *The Marechale,* by James Strachan

But are we not like men of a strange tongue when we talk to this generation about sacrifice? Our affluent Laodicean world is plagued by only one passion, the passion to possess. Does someone insist that it is poverty of *spirit* that is the important thing? We agree. That is the essential emphasis, whether we have little or much of this world's goods.

We are convinced, however, that some Christians will come to poverty of spirit through becoming dispossessed of property. Just as the rich young ruler was told to sell all and give all, so there are those today who, if they would have treasure in heaven, must go and give up—that trip, that sports car, that motorcycle, that unnecessary expense, in order to be foot free to follow their master, who was born in a stable, buried in a borrowed tomb, and all his life had not where to lay his head. Another such rich young man, after hearing a message on sacrificial giving, said: "It sent me back to college to live on half what I had lived on before."

An old soldier of the cross (under Hitler) said:

Every security in the world is a serious danger for the church of Christ. Everything that sets her on the path of faith is a wholesome gift. The fewer her outward means of help, the more genuine her love.

—*S. S. Times*

A loyal French soldier was being operated on. 'Twas in those days before surgery knew anaesthetics. As the doctor was probing to the bottom of the trouble, the patient responded: "Probe a little deeper, Doctor, and you will find the emperor." His majesty would be found at the heart of this warrior-soldier.

We have pointed out a few stakes of conviction that must needs be driven into the depths of our beings if ever we are to make any appreciable impact for Christ and his program for the lost world. As we submit to these stakes of conviction, we can respond with a sacrificial devotion that outstrips the French soldier: "Probe a little deeper, and at the heart of this warrior-soul you will find the Lord of all."

"If…" for Missionaries

(With apologies to Mr. Rudyard Kipling)

If you can hear God's call
When those about you
Are urging other calls and claims on you;
If you can trust your Lord when others doubt you,
Certain that he will guide you in all you do;
If you can keep your purpose with vision clear,
Bear lack of sympathy, yet sympathize,
Glimpsing his world task through your Savior's eyes.

If you can work in harmony with others,
Yet never lose your own distinctive aim,
Mindful that even among Christian brothers
Methods and plans are often not the same.
If you can see your cherished plan defeated,
And tactfully and bravely hold your peace,
And be undaunted when unfairly treated—
And pray that love and good will may increase.

If you can trust to native Christian brethren
The church you've built in lands across the sea,
Seeing in them, as your growing children,
Promises of the men that are to be;
If you can lead these eager weak beginners
By patient, loving care, your life, your prayer;

For failures and mistakes not judge as sinners,
But make their growth in grace your earnest care.

If you can share with humblest folk your virtue;
If nobler souls are richer for your touch;
If neither slight nor adulation hurt you;
If all men count with you, yet none too much;
If you can fill your most discouraged minute
With sixty seconds worth of patience true,
Yours is the task with all the challenge in it;
You'll be a missionary, through and through.

—Author Unknown

10

First Last and Last First

My late friend, Willis R. Hotchkiss, loved to tell thrilling accounts of his forty adventurous years in Africa.

One of the most remarkable stories he recounted is in connection with the two and a half years spent in order to find one word in the African's native tongue. He said he never appreciated the meaning of the word "Savior," until he found himself unable to use it with the natives. And how his heart was thrilled when on one memorable night the darkness of his understanding was suddenly illuminated. And how did it all come about?

A fellow missionary had been attacked and badly mauled by a lioness. Suddenly seizing the missionary, she had shaken him the way a cat plays with a mouse. But the nearby native servant, Kikuvi, shouted at that moment, and the lioness ran away to her cubs. That shout had delivered his master.

As Mr. Hotchkiss and Kikuvi sat about the campfire one evening, Kikuvi began to retell the story in great detail. Mr. Hotchkiss listened, all eyes and ears. He felt sure that out of this review would come that long-looked-for word, "Savior." But Mr. Hotchkiss became sick of heart and disappointed that night when, after such a long and detailed account of how Kikuvi had delivered his master, the word for "Savior" had apparently not been used.

But, suddenly, Kikuvi uttered just one sentence of only four words. He said, "I *saved* the master." There it was. Mr. Hotchkiss said, "That is the word I have been wanting. You *saved* your master." There and then the black face of Kikuvi lighted up with that light which never shone on land or sea. He saw how that God had so loved the world that he had given his only begotten Son to *save* us. The joy of Mr.

Hotchkiss knew no bounds. The jazz and follies of this world, he said, were in comparison like the crackling of thorns under a pot.

From our pulpit Mr. Hotchkiss tellingly related the cost of missionary effort in a heathen and savage land. Of the first twelve missionaries of the Africa Inland Mission he himself was the only one left after two and a half years. He was attacked by lions and rhinoceroses many times. He was compassed about by savage men with their poisoned arrows ready to strike him dead. For as long as fourteen months he never saw any bread. For months he lived on beans and sour milk. For many weeks he had no salt. He had to eat anything, all the way from ants to rhinoceros.

But I can still hear him say, "Do not talk to me about sacrifice. When I think of the superlative joy of uttering that one word, 'Savior,' and of proclaiming it to a great tribe who never heard it before, I never can think of those forty long years in terms of sacrifice."

Certainty of Reward

I would like to have you take your Bible and follow me in an exposition of Matthew 19:16 to 20:16. The rich young ruler had come asking, "Good master, what good thing shall I do, that I may have eternal life?" To that question the Savior laid down the following rigid conditions: "If thou wilt be perfect, go and sell that thou hast, and give to the poor, and thou shalt have treasure in heaven: and come and follow me." At that saying the young man went away sorrowful. Having failed to meet the conditions, he could *not have* what he sought, eternal life.

While Jesus was speaking to his disciples regarding things that grew out of the young ruler's departure, Peter began to reflect on how the rich young man had failed to qualify for life eternal. Peter raised a new question. "Then answered Peter and said unto Jesus: Lo, *we* have forsaken all, and have followed thee; what then shall we *have?*" Peter is saying, We have done what that rich young ruler did not do; what shall we have? What treasure shall we have as thy disciples? Master, did you promise that rich young man treasure hereafter if he would but leave all and follow thee? Now, master, we have done just that, we have been obedient, we have indeed left all to follow thee; what treasure, pray tell, shall we have for having left all?

Now note that Jesus did not despise Peter's question. In fact, he answered him with that strong word, "Verily." Then followed the promise: "Verily, I say unto you, That ye which have followed me, in the regeneration when the Son of man shall sit in the throne of his glory, ye also shall sit upon twelve thrones, judging the twelve tribes of Israel. And every one that hath forsaken houses, or brethren, or sisters, or father, or mother, or wife, or children, or lands, for my name's sake, shall receive an hundredfold, and shall inherit everlasting life. But many that are first shall be last; and the last shall be first" (Matt. 19:28–30).

Co-Rulers with Him

Christ plainly promised these disciples that when he himself had won the victory, and when his kingdom had been established, then they would be his co-rulers, sitting with him upon thrones and judging the twelve tribes of Israel. In substance, he is saying here what he says elsewhere, that there will be thrones to occupy, cities to rule, pounds and talents to be awarded. He is saying that God is not unrighteous to forget any man's work and labor of love; that the laborer is indeed worthy of his hire; that there will be crowns of righteousness, crowns of life, crowns of rejoicing, and crowns of glory. Rewards there will be even to an hundredfold.

Quality, Not Quantity

But notice next the Savior's word of warning: Many shall be last that are first, and first that are last. There is no break in the thought. Jesus then follows with the parable which closes with these words, "*So* the last shall be first, and the first last" (Matt. 20:16). Between these repeated statements regarding the last *first* and the first *last* lies the parable which relates to these statements. After warning the disciples that many shall be last that are first, and first that are last, then he gives that well-known parable and illustration of the laborers and the vineyard.

Keep in mind that Peter implied that the disciples should have a superior place over the rich young ruler. "Lo, *we have left all,* and have followed thee; what then shall we have?" That is to say, Some time ago we actually left all. We have been serving thee already after having left so much, after having left the all that the rich young ruler refused to leave. We are the very first of thy disciples to have left all. "What shall we have?"

Service and Reward

Now recall briefly the parable. It has to do with Christian disciples and their service and reward. The householder goes out early in the morning to hire laborers to work in his vineyard. He agrees with them for a penny a day. That is the bargain. At the third hour of the day he sends others into the vineyard promising them that which is "right." Again at the sixth hour, and the ninth hour and, finally, at the eleventh hour, he still promises that each will receive that which is right. At the close of the day the lord of the vineyard tells his steward to "call the laborers and give them their hire, beginning from the last unto the first."

Thus the steward began with those latecomers who entered the vineyard at the eleventh hour. Each of these received a penny. At the other end of the line stood those curious onlookers who had worked hard all day. They had been the first to enter the vineyard. We read that "when the first came, they supposed that they should have received more," but they received every man a penny. Then they began to murmur against the goodman of the house. Their complaint was this: "These last have spent but one hour, and thou hast made them equal unto us, who have borne the burden of the day and the scorching heat" (20:12 ASV).

Now the point of this parable is not to teach that the reward of one man will be the same as the reward of another. There is much Scripture to prove that there will be varying degrees of reward according to sacrificial, faithful, and long service. Rewards will be bestowed according to that which we have done, whether it be good or bad. This parable is not concerned with salvation, or with the varying rewards.

The purpose of this parable is one and one only. The point here is that a man's reward will be, not necessarily according to length of service, and most certainly not according to the number of talents and accomplishments, but according to the spirit and faithfulness to the opportunity given each disciple. The man who labored all day had his opportunity. Those who went out at the third hour, and the sixth hour, and the ninth hour, yea, even at the eleventh hour, each served according to his opportunity. As shown by his spirit and fidelity the eleventh-hour laborer was faithful to his opportunity.

Peter has been answered. He had questioned: "Behold, we have forsaken all, and followed thee; what shall we have therefore?" Jesus had promised his disciples and all such followers that to forsake all ensured reward even to "an hundredfold" in this life, to say nothing of the life to come. But then he warned Peter, and us all, that the latecomer, even at the eleventh hour, if he works faithfully right up to the close of its little day, will receive a reward equal to his opportunity.

Let me say without delay: Oh, the shocks and reversals and stunning revelations which will be experienced in that day when the keeper of the vineyard settles with us his laborers! We have been well warned that many shall be last that are first, and first that are last. The tables will be turned on that awful day when, in the next world, we behold that which we have never dreamed.

Peril of a Long Service

Now let me make a few observations. First of all, I would say that *long service can become a great peril*. While it is a great privilege and opportunity to have a long Christian life and long Christian service, that very privilege is freighted with the most frightful perils.

The very length of our service may lead to murmuring at the close of the day. "When the first came, they supposed that they should have received more." So many of God's hardworking servants, who have borne the burden of the day and the scorching heat, come to feel that they should receive more, both in time and in eternity. They have borne long and well; they have made their mark in God's vineyard; they have suffered much. Many of these old warriors have "gone through the mill" of fiery persecution and trial. Why should they not receive more—of recognition? Of respect? Of honor? Of reward? Of payment? And deference?

Their reasoning, as they line up for settlement, is this: Who are these eleventh-hour men, these latecomers, these that have spent but one hour? Shall these be made equal with us, who have borne the burden of the day and the scorching heat? Perish the thought! Have we no advantage over them? Let no one say that we, who have been "through the mill," have no more than they coming to us in the way of consideration and reward. Do you mean to tell us that this young Johnny-come-late shall be equal unto us?

Such is the peril of a long service. The lord of the vineyard sees all this and must often reverse the tables. The first goes down to the last, while the last comes up to the place of the first.

Some Examples of Reversal

The momentous principle embodied in the first last, and the last first, finds abundant illustration throughout the ages. The cases of Jacob and Esau embody this reversal of position. Esau, the elder, despised his birthright, and Jacob ascended to first place. Then listen to Esau's complaint: "Is not he rightly named Jacob? For he hath supplanted me these two times: he took away my birthright; and, behold, now he hath taken away my blessing."

In spite of the fact that many of the saints have scorned Jacob's methods, let us remember that the Savior made it a great privilege to sit down in the Kingdom of Heaven with Abraham, Isaac, and *Jacob*. And, indeed, said the Savior, "They shall come from the east, and from the west, and from the north, and from the south, and shall sit down in the kingdom of God. And, behold, there are last which shall be first, and there are first which shall be last" (Luke 13:29-30).

This interchange of destiny finds perfect illustration also in the case of Ishmael and Isaac. Ishmael is the firstborn, born some fourteen years before Isaac. When a great feast is made for Isaac, the heir of promise, behold Ishmael standing on the sideline "mocking." The flesh envies and mocks the Spirit. As then, he that was born after the flesh persecuted him that was born after the Spirit; even so it is now. But Isaac supplants Ishmael. Ishmael shall not be heir with Isaac.

I cannot but note how easy it is for men who have begun in the Spirit to end in the flesh. Many, who have been first to enter the race, have been the last to breast the tape. Men of God who have been first in service and sacrifice, and who have been born in persecution and baptized in blood, have in time become so self-satisfied and sure of their position and advantage that they have become cold and calculating and complaining. They murmur against any least suggestion that the eleventh-hour latecomer should even be thought "equal" to them. They bear in their body, not only the burden and heat of the day, but, perhaps, "the marks of the Lord Jesus." But longevity of service ensures neither priority nor place.

Consider again the testimony of Mr. Hotchkiss after having borne the burden and heat of many years in the heart of hot, hot Africa: "Do not talk to me about sacrifice. When I think of the superlative joy of uttering that one word 'Savior,' and proclaiming it to a great tribe who never heard it before, I never can think of those forty long years in terms of sacrifice." David Livingstone likewise felt that the long-time suffering missionary should never think of his labor in terms of "sacrifice."

Lengthy service, therefore, need not jeopardize one's reward. *The first need not be last.* Though there be great peril attached to lengthy and laborious service, the long-time servant is not pre-appointed to defeat. He who begins well and runs well to the end of the race will be crowned "in due time" with glory and honor. Just beware of being soured before the sunset of service.

Complaint, or Contrition?

I know of a missionary couple who passed through a frightful career in a concentration camp in the Far East and came out still carnal. They came out to seek, for their children, place and culture and position in the world. The concentration camp could not correct what the cross could not cure. It is perilously possible to bear the burden of the day of persecution, and the scorching heat of near-martyrdom, and yet come forth unclean, and murmuring that others should be "made equal."

This murmuring disciple also finds perfect illustration in the elder brother of Luke 15. When the prodigal son returns repentant and is clothed and feasted with the fatted calf, the elder son begins to murmur against the father. Listen to his complaint: "Lo, these many years do I serve thee, neither transgressed I at any time thy commandment: and yet thou never gavest me a kid, that I might make merry with my friends: But as soon as this thy son was come, which hath devoured thy living with harlots, thou hast killed for him the fatted calf."

The elder brother cannot appreciate the prodigal's tears, his repentance, his confession of sin, his conversion. All this he despises. All he knows is a kind of half-hearted routine and legalistic service. He knows nothing of a broken spirit and a contrite heart.

He never makes one little move to go and bring the younger prodigal home. As far as the elder brother is concerned, let the younger son die in the hog pen. Little does he care if the lost lad never comes home! He partakes of the spirit of another elder brother. When God asked Cain: "Where is Abel thy brother?" the murderer retorted: "I know not: Am I my brother's keeper?" (Gen. 4:9). The spirit of the elder brother was akin to that of Cain. He was anti-missionary. Instead of saying, "Am I my brother's keeper?" Cain should have said, "Am I *not* my brother's keeper?"

But take care my "elder brother." Take heed to your spirit. We, too, can be anti-missionary. You and I can sit in our "comfortable pew" of privilege and leave prodigal people to their eternal fate, caring little if millions die far from home. Are we not our brother's keeper? Yet most of us could not care less about his everlasting lostness. The lostness of the lost has not gripped us. We can be as loveless as Cain or as the elder brother in leaving prodigal people to their hopeless lot, unconcerned if they never get home. Cain was a murderer, deliberate and high-handed. Our crime is irresponsibility—murder by neglect.

Remember, O elder brother of mine, that the day is not far distant when the well behaved and highly favoured, who never at any time broke their Father's commandment, will be disinherited and will behold others who will "come from the east, and from the west, and from the north, and from the south, and shall sit down in the kingdom of God. And, behold, (to our consternation) there are last (heathen and prodigals) who shall be first, and there are first (in favor and privilege) who shall be last" (Luke 13:29-30). The interchange of destiny may be repeated. But let us return to the trusting first-love of the eleventh-hour laborer. It is happy-hearted and hilarious service that satisfies the master.

Someone has well said concerning the all-day laborers in the vineyard, *"They that bargained got what they bargained for; but they that trusted got more than heart could conceive."* How true! How blessedly true! Those who began early in the day agreed to work for one penny for the day. They got what they bargained for. What complaint had they?

What Was Your Bargain?

Now let me ask the preacher or parent or missionary or Sunday school teacher: Did you not start out in early life to forsake all? Yea, even houses and brethren, and sisters, and father, and mother, and children, and lands for his name's sake? Was not that your bargain? Did you not consecrate all, hoping for nothing in return? Trot along, take your wages and get going. Why this murmuring against the goodman of the house? Why should you now suppose you should receive more? Don't you see that something has happened in your soul? Something has made you sour. You have begun to lose your keen sense of appreciation of the privilege of sacrifice. Even from the standpoint of justice you have no complaint. You have received what you bargained for.

Think how different is the spirit of the eleventh-hour laborers: "They that trusted got more than heart could conceive." Those last-hour laborers, delighted and happy with the privilege, redeemed the time, bought up the opportunity, threw themselves into their labor, and trusted the goodman of the house. It is this happy and carefree confidence that the lord of the vineyard loves to reward. With the spirit of that great soldier, Napoleon, they cried: "There is time to win a battle before the sun goes down." "They that bargained got what they bargained for; but they that (hilariously and happily) trusted got more than heart could conceive." The first are last, the last are first.

At the close of the Civil War in America the army that passed through Georgia was to be reviewed in one of the great cities. Then there was to be a parade. The night before the parade General Sherman called General Howard to his tent and said: "General, you are one of the men who marched with me through Georgia. You are to ride at the head of your division tomorrow in the parade. But a plan is being pressed that another general should precede you in the event he is to take over the leadership in the division. I hardly know what to do inasmuch as political motive sometimes is stronger than personal right. I don't know how to meet this difficulty."

Very naturally General Howard said, "Well, I think I am entitled to ride at the head of my division. It was I who led them to victory."

General Sherman replied, "You are entitled to it, but I am wondering whether Christian consideration may not influence you to make an exception in this case, waive your personal rights, and let the other man go at the head of your division, simply for the sake of peace—not that it is fair to you."

"Oh," said General Howard, "if it is a matter of Christian consideration, I yield; he may have my place."

"Very well," said General Sherman, "I will so arrange, and will you report to me tomorrow morning at nine o'clock? *You shall ride with me at the head of the army.*"

General Howard bore the burden and heat of the day of battle, voluntarily lost all, and *was still first*. The Savior did not say, *all* the first shall be last, and *all* the last first. He said, Many. General Howard remained first, one of the few.

The Day Is Short

Recall once again the heart-warming words of Mr. Hotchkiss after forty years of burden-bearing and scorching heat:

I never can think of those forty years in terms of sacrifice—don't talk to me about sacrifice.

He did not suppose that he should "receive more." Those who trust receive more than heart could wish. Let all bargainers beware.

Surely it is the eleventh hour. Or is it the twelfth? Beyond dispute the hour is late. It may be much later than we think. The world's midnight hastens on apace—when no man can work. How short is our little day of opportunity! Many millions in darkness are still awaiting an army of eleventh-hour laborers. As we consider the darkening condition of our homelands, our darkness is almost white by comparison with the regions beyond. A zealous missionary says, "The need here at home is only a drop in the ocean as compared to the needs out there."

Let me address my young reader friend: "Why stand ye here all the day idle? For, if you are not doing your utmost to win the lost, are you not virtually 'idle'? Move out! Get going! Go ye into the vineyard! Many that are *last* shall be *first.*"

There is time for you, latecomer though you be, to win a battle before your sun goes down!

Those Excused from Going

Those who believe that the world is not lost and does not need a Savior.

Those who believe that Jesus Christ made a mistake when he said: "Go ye into all the world, and preach the gospel to every creature."

Those who believe that the gospel is not the power of God, and cannot save the heathen.

Those who wish that missionaries had never come to our ancestors, and that we ourselves were still heathen.

Those who believe that it is "every man for himself" in this world, and who, with Cain, ask, "Am I my brother's keeper?"

Those who want no share in the final victory of Christ.

Those who believe they are not accountable to God for the money entrusted to them.

Those who are prepared to accept the final sentence: "Inasmuch as ye did it not to one of the least of these, ye did it not to me."

—Horace Bushnell

11

Have Me Excused

When Christians come to facing up to missionary obligation and obedience, there are many ways of saying: "I pray thee have me excused." Frankly, are there not multitudes of Christian young men and women who have no real or sufficient reason for not going abroad as missionaries? But many of them begin "with one consent to make excuse." We believe it has been well said that an excuse is "a skin of a reason stuffed with a lie."

We would introduce our discussion on excuse making by listening to a great pioneer among the Muslims of Arabia. Ion Keith-Falconer was a Scottish nobleman and a brilliant Cambridge scholar who forfeited fame and fortune in order to reach destitute Muslims with the gospel. After only two years, repeated fevers sapped his strength and took his frail life. But he left us this convicting missionary challenge:

> While vast continents still lie shrouded in almost utter darkness and hundreds of millions suffer the horrors of heathenism and Islam, the burden of proof rests on you to show that the circumstances in which God has placed you were meant to keep you out of the foreign mission field.

In this chapter we want to deal briefly with some of the more common excuses voiced as an escape from personal involvement in God's great missionary enterprise. The content of this book is meant to furnish pastors and Christian workers with Biblical material to stir God's people out of their evangelical smugness. Do we not all need to be stabbed wide awake?

Missionary-minded pastors know that "the *going* church is the *growing* church." The wise pastor will therefore do everything in his power to keep the missionary program uppermost in his ministry. As pastors we cannot take missions for granted. On the one hand, we must present facts and figures from foreign fields; but we must also preach Bible-based sermons on missions, or missionary fires will die down among our people. And we must, withal, put away all kinds of keen and subtle excuse-making on the part of both parents and their young people. May this chapter assist pastors and parents and evangelical leaders to deal a death blow to every crafty excuse lurking in the minds of prospective recruits.

We are deeply indebted to the Rev. J. Heywood Horsburgh, a great missionary warrior who once listed and answered some fifty common excuses regarding missionary involvement. We have made abundant use of his material, sometimes within quotes, sometimes without due credit.

1. I do not believe in missions to the heathen. They are absurd.

If you are not a Christian, who would expect you to believe in missions? Why should you? How could you? To "the natural man" the things of the Spirit are "absurd" indeed, "foolishness." Paul says, "neither can he know them" (1 Cor. 2:14).

The first principle of missions means acceptance of Christ. If you have rejected God's great Missionary himself, how could you be a hearty advocate of missions? Until you bow the knee to Christ, you can only think of missions as of no use—only a waste of time, a waste of money, a waste of effort. Of course your argument is with the Master, who (according to your theory) made a mistake in coming to this world to save lost men, and made a further blunder in commissioning his servants to go into all the world to preach the gospel.

If, however, you are a real Christian, how can you say you do not believe in missions? How can you believe in him and yet dispute his parting command? Jesus said: "If ye love me, ye will keep my commandments" (John 14:15 ASV). How can any man be a consistent Christian and not believe in missions? Do you not believe in your own salvation? And when Christ comes again and begins to reckon with his servants, will you want to be found among those who did not believe in doing what he bids them?

2. God is so merciful that the heathen will not be lost. Everything will turn out all right for them in the end.

By what authority do you say the heathen will not be lost? Scriptures make it plain, especially Romans 1 and 2 and many other such chapters, that men everywhere are *already lost*—lost without God, without Christ, and without hope (see Appendix E).

God is indeed merciful, but he is also holy and just. And the heathen for the most part already know they are wicked and unfit for heaven—"who (know) the judgment of God, that they which commit such things are worthy of death" (Rom. 1:32).

Dr. Henry Frost recounted an instance of a missionary coming upon a heathen chief in the heart of Africa who had never seen a white man, had never read the Bible, and had never heard the gospel. After a casual and friendly conversation with the chief, it suddenly occurred to the missionary that it was a good opportunity to test the question of the heathen conscience. The following conversation took place, the missionary asking the questions and the chieftain answering them:

"Is it wrong to lie?"

"Yes, it is wrong to lie."

"Is it wrong to steal?"

"Yes, it is wrong to steal."

"Is it wrong to commit adultery?"

"Yes, it is very wrong to commit adultery."

"Is it wrong to commit murder?"

The chieftain, at this, looked closely at the missionary and said, "Do you take me for a fool?"

Here was a man who knew nothing about God's revealed law or the later revelation of the New Testament, but who had the sum and substance of the law written in the mind and conscience by the Holy Spirit. Dr. Frost goes on to say:

> At the same time, no doubt, he lied a hundred times a day, stole whenever he could, had twenty or thirty wives, some of whom had been other men's wives, and had committed so many murders that he would have

found it difficult to remember them. In other words, he knew the law, but had not kept it, which is the condition in lesser or greater measure, of all the heathen.

Let the reader make a fresh study of Scripture and accept its plain and solemn verdict regarding the state of the heathen, whether East or West, and there will come the conviction that will result in expanded missionary effort.

3. We should not go and preach against other religions, or give the impression that we think we are the only ones that are right.

Again we must think within the Scriptures. We dare "not think … above that which is written" (1 Cor. 4:6). We grant that there is such a study as that of comparative religions, but Christianity does not happen to be one of them. Scripture makes it plain as day that all heathen religions, in spite of the few ethical sayings found among them, are substitute contraptions of the Devil to blind and bind men in chains of darkness.

We do not go abroad to preach against false religions. We preach Christ. When the converts "turn to God from idols" (1 Thess. 1:9), they burn their own gods just as saved sinners in this country confess and forsake their sins.

We don't just *think* we are the only ones who are right. We *"know* him whom we have believed" (2 Tim. 1:12 ASV). Do we sound dogmatic? We are, but our boast is only of him who said: *"I am the way, the truth, and the life; no man cometh unto the Father but by me"* (John 14:6). We are so intolerant of substitute religion, of every falsification of the truth, that we don't waste time debating about which is the right religion. Let those debate who have only some religion to debate about. We have something far better than religion. In fact, religion was one of those things we got delivered from when we got saved from all sin. We now have a living Lord and Savior who saves men, not *in* their sins but *from* their sins.

Without apology or fear of contradiction, we boldly charge all natural religion as being the culprit profaning the temple of the Most High God. And as such it has defaced the human soul and stripped its victims of every trace of the divine. All the light of false religion is but a will-o'-the-wisp. "Her gaudy garments, be they garish or somber gray, smell of brimstone and the pit" (Wilkes).

4. The heathen do not want us to come preaching to them. They have their religion and are quite satisfied with it.

Here are things right and wrong. Who wants to be preached to if he is told what a guilty sinner he is? People at home do not like it, either. But there are some, both at home and abroad, who are sick of sin's bondage and do want to be told the way of deliverance through Christ.

But what about the heathen being happy with their little false religion? This is another threadbare excuse that ignores the facts as anyone acquainted with the heathen world well knows. "The dark places of the earth are full of the habitations of cruelty" (Psa. 74:20). Who can be happy who is blind and bruised and broken and beaten, and who "through fear of death is all his lifetime subject to bondage"? While hugging his chains, how can the slave be happy in his captivity?

> Thou art chained to the wheel of the foe
> By ties that a world cannot sever;
> With thy tyrant through storm and through calm
> thou shalt go,
> And thy sentence is bondage forever.

5. What presumption for us to go to highly civilized people like the Japanese and the Chinese and those of Central Europe and force our opinions upon them!

Man looks on the outward appearance, but God looks on the heart. All civilized people, both at home and abroad, have been fatally bitten by the serpent of sin and stand in equal need of Christ. Civilized men of the heathen world may be dressed in gaudy Western garb of the latest fashion, while at the same time they continue to prostrate themselves in their temples before those senseless idols. It matters not whether those idols be of Buddha in Japan, the icons of Greek orthodoxy, the virgin of Italy, the crucifix of Quebec or France, or the money and materialism of America. The most advanced civilization stalks abroad hand in hand with varying but equally degrading forms of idolatry. Apart from Christ no one has any cure. Any and all must behold the uplifted Lord and Savior as the one and only remedy.

We do not force our opinions upon men, whether they be civilized or uncivilized. Our opinions, no better than theirs, will do them no good. They just need Christ to save them from their cultured respectability, their self-righteousness, their civilized heathenism.

6. **The Gentile nations object to our use of the term "heathen," implying that we of the Western nations are Christian.**

In a sense they are right. But the fact is that any man without Christ in the East is no more of a heathen than any unconverted individual in the West. It should be understood that there is no such thing as a Christian nation today, and it is wrong to give any other nation that impression of us.

The term "Gentile" means "heathen" in the New Testament. In Old Testament times all peoples other than God's people, Israel, were known as the "nations."

7. **If the heathen act up to the light they have they will be all right and will be saved by their religions.**

We might ask: How many people in the homeland act up to the light they have? If they did, they would come to Christ. But how shall the heathen believe on him of whom they have not heard? Let every disputer first answer Paul's four "hows" of Romans 10:14 and 15, and we can thereafter discuss some of the difficult questions regarding the light which the heathen already have through creation and conscience.

It was Dan Crawford, the great missionary of the dark continent, who said: "The heathen in the heart of Africa is sinning against a flood of light."

In the meantime, let us remember that any substitute religion can save no sinner from his sins, no drunkard from his drink, no miser from his money, no harlot from her shame, no proud man from his pride, no Pharisee from his self-righteousness. No form of religion, not even the Christian form, can save any sinner. But only our crucified and living Savior can save and does save the heathen, even the chief of sinners.

8. I believe there are plenty of heathen in this country. Charity begins at home.

Indeed there are heathen here, too many of them. Whether at home or abroad there are always heathen who will not accept the gospel. As it was in Paul's day so it is now: "Some believed ... and some believed not" (Acts 28:24). But shall we confine our preaching to gospel-hardened people here, instead of giving others over there a chance to hear? Why should any man hear the gospel twice before another man has a chance to hear it once? (Smith). Remember that your relatives and mine, your lost ancestors and mine, would have had no gospel apart from a foreign missionary. Yes, charity begins at home, but it does not stay at home.

Charles Simeon of the great Cambridge pulpit was the spiritual father of the great Henry Martyn, mentioned elsewhere in this book. Let me give one brief quotation as recorded by Bishop Moule:

> It may be asked, perhaps, why are we to waste our strength upon the heathen? Is there not scope for the labors of all at home? I answer, "It is well for us that the apostles did not argue thus; for if they had not turned to the Gentiles till there remained no unconverted Jews, the very name of Christ would probably long since have been forgotten among men.
>
> Besides, the more our love abounds toward the heathen, the more will the zeal of others be provoked for the salvation of our neighbors; and the more confidently may we hope for the blessing of God upon their pious endeavors. Then let all excuses be put away, and let all exert themselves at least in prayer to the great "Lord of the harvest," and entreat him day and night, "to send forth laborers into his harvest."

9. I do not encourage my son or daughter to be a missionary.

So you wish them to be excused. Would it not be better to have your child abroad in the will of God than living at home in disobedience? You would gladly wed your child to an earthly mate. Can you not give him or her to Christ for his service? Can you not trust the one who died for both you and your offspring? You believe that God "spared not his only Son, but delivered him up for us all." Abraham "offered up his only begotten son." Can you not then as a Christian parent deliver up your child for his service? Let God's unspared love in giving his only Son be your model and motivation.

10. Not everybody can be a missionary. Some good Christians must keep the home fires burning.

Right you are—in part. Not everyone should be a foreign missionary. But we keep plenty of good Christians at home. If only one out of a thousand goes abroad, what are we so anxious about? And if 90 per cent of the world's peoples get less than 10 per cent of God's servants, surely our mouths should be stopped for very shame and selfishness. Out of fairness to the lost of heathen lands let this proportion be reversed before ever we begrudge the heathen one out of a thousand.

11. This business of missions belongs to missionaries. I can't be too concerned.

Alexander Duff, the great Scottish missionary, said: "There was a time when I had no care or concern for the heathen. That was the time I had no care for my own soul. But by the grace of God when I began to care for my own soul, I began to care for the heathen, too. And in my closet on bended knees I said: 'Oh, Lord, thou knowest silver and gold have I none for this cause. What I have I give; I offer myself; wilt thou accept the gift?'"

If you belong to Christ, you are his servant. You should do his bidding; his business is your business. His concern for the "other sheep" should be your concern. He said, "Them also I must bring." But without your help and mine how can he "bring them in"? You and I are the one indispensable link. Once you become involved as a copartner with the missionary in his business, the chances are you may become a volunteer for the field. In any case find your part in God's plan of missions—then do it.

12. I would not mind going to the missionary front if there are no difficult circumstances, but I do not want to run any risks.

Fine talk indeed for a soldier! Imagine a recruit in Her Majesty's forces quite willing to go to the front if there be no difficulties, no dangers and no risks to be taken. Paul called for good soldiery on Timothy's part. "Take thy share in suffering hardship as a true soldier of Christ Jesus" (2 Tim. 2:3).

13. What will happen when I get too old to be a missionary? I want to know your retirement policy.

Think of Christ's promise to his missionary servants: "Lo, I am with you *all the days* (Matt. 28:20). God's promises are: "Even to your old age I am he: and even to hoar hairs will I carry you." "I the Lord, the first, and with the last" (Isa. 46:4; 41:4). Surely these passages about God's care are as dependable as John 3:16 and Romans 8:28. "Do not be anxious then, saying, What shall we eat? … for your heavenly Father knows that you need all these things" (Matt. 6:31-32, NASB).

But it is well that you sit down now and count the cost, whether you have sufficient to finish this discipleship. One candidate who was anxious about the society's retirement policy was told: "Yes, brother, we have a little plot of ground in the rear of our mission station where our missionaries retire." That was a good reply to a delicate disciple.

14. I am not fit to be a missionary. I have not been to college.

Of course you are not fit. If you thought you were, it would be the sure sign that you are not. God's supreme qualification is weakness: "When I am weak, then am I strong" (2 Cor. 12:10). God chooses the things that "are not." It sounds as though you qualify for that category.

As to college, never mind. College is not essential. Look at the early disciples—"ignorant and unlearned men." But knowledge of God's Word is primary. If you are willing, humble, teachable, and bent on *serving* instead of *shining*, you can be useful as a missionary.

"There is a place for a college education, but that is at the pierced feet of Christ. It is legitimate if it leads directly to the fulfilment of God's will in a person's life. But it is utterly wrong if its aim is to equip a Christian to make a name for himself in the world, or to waste his time and energy chasing the baubles of earthly advantage. It is all right if it can be chained to the chariot wheels of God, but should be counted as dung if it lures a man away from the primary to the trivial."[1]

15. I have no special gifts or talents.

God needs some common foot soldiers. Too many are ambitious to be captains. Dr. A. B. Simpson once said: "There are not many great rivers in the world, but there are many little rivers that run into other rivers." You may feel like a little creek, but you may make a contribution to the onflow of God's more gifted servants. Ask God for the gift of "helps" (1 Cor. 12:28). Little is much if God is in it. Every little helps.

Some special gifts are necessary and useful, but they are not primary. William Carey, the gifted father of modern missions, commenting with reference to his life's accomplishment said, "There is nothing remarkable in it; it has only required perseverance ... if anyone gives me credit for being a plodder, he will do me justice. Anything beyond this will be too much. I can plod. I can persevere in any definite pursuit. To this I owe everything."

Years ago a missionary leader said: "The crying need in China today (he might have said India or Africa or South America) is for hundreds of ordinary people filled with the Spirit of God."

---

1. From *Grasping for Shadows*, by Wm. MacDonald. Walterick Publishers. By permission.

And another God-owned spiritual leader said:

> The need of the mission field is not more money, or more education, or more brains; still less is it more organization or more method.
>
> It is spiritual leadership, and spiritual leadership is not won or established by promotion, but by many prayers, and tears, and confessions of sin, and heart-searchings, and humblings before God, and self-surrender, and a courageous sacrifice of every idol, and a bold and deathless and uncompromising, uncomplaining embracing of the cross, and an eternal, unfaltering looking unto Jesus crucified …. Spiritual leaders are not made by man, nor any combination of men. Neither conferences nor synods nor councils can make them, but only God.

16. I have no great love for the heathen.

Christ never asked Peter if he loved the *sheep*. He asked him if he loved his *Lord*. "If you love *me*, ye will keep my commandments" (John 14:15 ASV). His command is "Feed my sheep." "Go, tell." Love will spring up as you obey Christ's command. God's love will be shed abroad in your heart by the Holy Ghost, which is given unto you. But remember that God gives the Holy Ghost to them that obey him.

17. I am willing to go

Willingness is good, but it is not enough! Faith without works is dead. Willingness without action is fruitless. Year after year some young fellow stands up as a volunteer: "Here am I," he says—"Yea, still here!" Why not cry out in desperation, "Lord, *send me.*" Get some push and go in your bosom and in your boots.

James Chalmers of New Guinea, martyred and eaten by cannibals after thirty-one years of sacrificial service, once expressed willingness plus action when he said:

> Here I am, Lord, send me; send me to the ends of the earth; send me to the rough and savage pagans of the wilderness; send me from all that is called comfort in the earth; send me even to death itself; if it be but in thy service, and to promote thy Kingdom.

18. I'll make money and send others.

Splendid! If that is what God wants you to do. And that is exactly what God wants more of his servants to do. But if you are young enough to go, be sure you are not using this plea as an excuse for not going yourself. To many a self-excusing candidate God has said: "I don't want your *money;* I want *you.*" First you, then your money. The poor Macedonians set the example for all true giving. They "first gave their own selves to the Lord"; then to others "by the will of God" (2 Cor. 8:5). God wants first our *persons,* then our *purses.*

19. I don't feel the Lord wants me to be a missionary.

How were you saved? By faith, or by feeling? It was by trusting Christ and not by feeling that you became his child. Now you are to serve Christ by obeying his commands and not by consulting your "feelings." As a Christian, you must keep these three words before you, and in this order: facts, faith, feelings. Faith follows facts and lets feelings trail along. Keep looking at the facts of God's Word, facts regarding God's love for the heathen, their crying need of Christ, and the Master's command to go. Let your faith be a faith that obeys God's Word. Feelings are always treacherous. Those who go by feelings make shoddy Christians.

Abraham did not feel like leaving his home country but "by faith Abraham … obeyed," and "he went out, not knowing whither" (Heb. 11:8). Later, when he climbed mount Moriah with his only begotten son, it was only "by faith Abraham … offered up … Isaac" (Heb. 11:17). We may be sure that it was not by feelings the patriarch ascended that mount of supreme consecration.

Such is God's purpose for us too, to go forth into new service, to push out and upward and onward. Alas, how often we stand still and idle, never expecting to be thrust out into new fields of labor, of conquest, of trial, and of triumph. But all must be by faith, faith in Christ's Word of promise.

How the heart of the true Christian rejoices as he reads of the victories of faith in foreign lands—of the revivals in Korea, Uganda, Indonesia, Kenya, Brazil, and other parts of the earth, and delights in the names of Gilmour, Morrison, Brainerd, Martyn, Duff, Livingstone, Moffat, Paton, Chalmers, Hudson Taylor, Bingham, Judson, Goforth, Carey, Jaffray, and many another mighty leader who, like Abraham, "went forth, not knowing whither he went," heard the summons and promise of God, and pushed forward, not by feelings, but by the power of faith.

Of course you may not feel like being a missionary. But the habitual use of the phrase, "I don't feel like it," is the mark of a weakling, not of a strong Christian. When a student sought to excuse himself for not having attended the final class session because he "didn't feel like it," his teacher replied: "Young man, has it ever occurred to you that the most of the world's work is done by people who don't feel like it?"

20. I believe I should have a special call to go.

The command to "Go" has been given. Have you had a special call to "Stop"? Christ's *command* is behind you. The *need* of the heathen is before you. If you have no valid reason for not going, the "special call" you are looking for has already been given. When people are known to be perishing in a flood or in a fire, a man must hasten to the rescue instead of waiting for a call. Note the special chapter, "A Missionary Call," in *A Spiritual Clinic* by J. Oswald Sanders.

21. I am being so used here at home that I gather that I must stay here.

Do you conclude that God wants as missionaries only those who are failures here at home? "Is to be unsuccessful at home a good qualification for making a successful foreign missionary? Are we to offer our service to God for the heathen only when we find it is of no use elsewhere?"

Philip was in the heart of a great revival in Samaria when God called him to leave it and go to the desert to lead one man, the Ethiopian eunuch, to Christ (see Acts 8:26–40). Elisha was busy at the head of his father's ranch when God led him to higher service.

If you were unstable in this country, God would not likely want you to go abroad, at least not in that condition. To be usable *here* is to be usable *there*. Crossing the ocean will not make a successful missionary.

22. I must wait for God to close doors behind me and to open the door in front of me.

You may wait in vain. If you can be used abroad, all kinds of home folk will offer you open doors. And the front door may seem as fast closed as the Red Sea was before Israel. But "the Lord said unto Moses, Speak unto the children of Israel that they go forward." And as we go prayerfully forward one step at a time in the "obedience of faith," God marvelously opens the door—often beyond all we could ask or think. The great secret is "moment-by-moment" confidence, and "step-by-step" obedience.

Adoniram Judson was offered an attractive call to Park Street Church of Boston, but his answer was to this effect: "My work cannot be *here*, but *there*," and he became the great apostle to found the kingdom of God in Burma.

I recall a young recruit, aflame for God, who prayed: "Lord, you had better bar any door that you don't want me to go through, because I'm going." And she went to South America and did a splendid work for God.

23. I am too old to be a missionary. I could not learn the language.

This may or may not be true. You may be too old for some countries. But you might be able to go to a country where your own language is spoken, and for a short term. Ramon Llull, noble martyr for Christ, went as a missionary to the Muslims for the first time when he was 56 years of age, and for the third time when he was 79. At the age of 80 (in 1315) he was stoned to death. "In an age of violence he was the apostle of heavenly love." Let his own great motto be adopted by us all, regardless of our years: "He who loves not, lives not; he who lives by the Life cannot die."

24. I aim to help missions a little, but my little counts for next to nothing in a large missionary society.

Don't be too sure. We repeat: "Little is much when God is in it." God's work is supported largely by the many mites of God's poor, rather than with the large bank notes of the few rich.

Think of the poor widow. The Savior took stock of her gift, rather than the big gifts of the rich. Hers was "more than they all." Are you a little giver? Be encouraged. God measures our stewardship, not by what we give, but by what we have left.

25. If I don't go, God will get someone else to do my job, even though I'll miss the blessing. God can get his work done without me.

That excuse sounds almost like humility. But it's a specious bit of sophistry. Missionary appeals to young people for service often follow this kind of misleading and false reasoning. While we grant that there are multitudes of saints who miss the blessing of complete obedience to Christ's command (many of them "reaping corruption" even in this life), it is with the first part of this argument that we are here concerned. If it be true that "God will get someone else to do your job," how is it that over half of the world does not have the gospel? It is apparent that God is not getting someone else to do your work.

Christ's rule for his household servants, according to His own statement, is: "To every man *his* work." He did not say, To every man *some* work, or to each man a work, but "to every man *his work*"—to each his own particular task (see Mark 13:34 ASV). How then can another man do your work? If he does "his work," will he not be engaged full time? Will he not have all he can do? Face it! If you do not do your own work, who will? My friend, Christ is counting on you, counting on me. He has no other plan, for the simple reason that there is no other plan.

It may sound very spiritual for you to say, "God can get his work done without you or me"; but there is much subtle self-excusing in that high-sounding sentence. We repeat the question: How is it that such a vast amount of the world is without the gospel? Is this all God's fault? Or is there such a thing as criminal neglect and blood-guiltiness on man's part? Such irresponsibility classes us with Cain, who excused himself by retorting: "Am I my brother's keeper?"

If that is my self-chosen company, then I can join hands with the venerable moderator of the Nottingham meeting of Baptist ministers who answered William Carey's earnest appeal for sending the gospel to the heathen with the rebuke: "Sit down, young man. You are a miserable enthusiast to raise such a question. When God wants to convert the heathen, he will do it without your help or mine."

How good that William Carey's heart outran the Baptist deacon's doctrine! To India he went in obedience to Christ's missionary mandate, and thereby became the father of the modern missionary movement.

Excuses might be multiplied. But what shall we more say? We would plead with any possible candidate who is still young enough to get to the regions beyond: "If God is giving you the opportunity now, and you let it slip, he may never offer you the chance again. Some of us for whom it was possible to go to the heathen almost shudder to think *how nearly we stayed at home!*"

Listen to this touching request from a clergyman, eloquent in its sadness, recently made to a missionary bishop: "Pray for one who had the opportunity to go to the foreign field, but did not avail himself of it, and now when he would go, he cannot!" Oh, I beseech you, do not let this great matter drift. Do not walk in uncertainty. Do not be turned aside. You will be eternally the poorer if you do. (The above quotes are from Dr. Horsburgh, from whom we have freely quoted.)

A hundred years ago the church of Christ did practically nothing. Today a part of the church of Christ does—what is convenient! Think this over, and you will find it is true. It is myself, my home for myself, my children for myself, my church for myself, my country for myself—all these come first; the unevangelized nations are of little concern to us.

Yet, if this great work of evangelizing the world has really been entrusted to us—and who can listen to Christ and his own Bible and say that it has not—we ought to be bending all our energies to this task, making greater sacrifices as soldiers for its speedy accomplishment, making greater sacrifices than ever men do for their Queen and country....

But what sacrifices are we making? Were anybody to suggest that the church of Christ is seriously troubling itself about the evangelization of the world, he could only provoke a smile. Nay, has the thought of taking this task seriously ever entered our heads? What are we *doing?* What does it amount to? Far, far from realizing what a great work has been entrusted to us and rising *en masse* to grapple with it—as we ought to be doing—we are full of other thoughts, and plans, and works, generally narrow, too often selfish; and what we do to evangelize the world is mere byplay!

How shall we ever overcome our excuse-making? How awaken from our inertia—"that inertia that is so fatal on the eve of battle"? Let us be forever done with all excuses, but how? Where shall we begin? That is simple. Just begin. Act. Awaken to the next thing in the path of known duty. Walk in the light. Act out your faith. Keep up repeated acts of faith. Put faith to work.

Above all, do something—that next thing. Do it today—here and now. Keep on. Keep on keeping on. Go forth—anywhere, providing it be forward. Cry aloud. Spare not. Be earnest. Be hot for God. And then hotter. Stir into flame the gift that is in thee. Refuse all deadly indifference. Beware of the cooling-off process.

Spare yourself no pains. Go and sell and give. Speak and sing. Pray and testify. Keep your heart in heaven and your head in the Book. Put your hand to the plow—and the purse. Push the battle. Let your very talk, day in and day out, tell for eternity. "You have your Bibles and your knees," use them both—continually. Henry Martyn, after his first two days in India, wrote, "Now to burn out for God."

Begin to burn. Be a burning as well as a shining light. Remember that the missionary call is a call to battle, to conflict, to war. Above all, it is a prayer battle. Therefore set out to pray for missions and missionaries.

Listen to one who spoke from experience: "I want you to spend fifteen minutes every day praying for foreign missions," said a leader of God's people to his young folk. "But beware how you pray, for I warn you that it is a very costly experiment."

"Costly?" they asked in surprise.

"Aye, costly," he cried. "When Carey began to pray for the conversion of the world, it cost him himself, and it cost those who prayed with him very much. David Brainerd prayed for the dark-skinned savages, and after two years of blessed work, it cost him his life. Be sure it is a dangerous thing to pray in earnest for this work; you will find that you cannot pray and withhold labor, or pray and withhold your money; nay, that your very life will no longer be your own when your prayers begin to be answered."

Appendix A

The Right Use of Money
by John Wesley

The introduction of money into the world is one instance of the wise and gracious providence of God. "The love of money," we know from God's Word, "is the root of all evil"; but not the thing itself. The fault does not lie in the money, but in them that use it. It is as applicable to the best, as to the worst uses. It is of unspeakable service to all civilized nations, in all the common affairs of life; the instrument of transacting all manner of business and (if we use it according to Christian wisdom) of doing all manner of good.

It is therefore of the highest concern that all who fear God know how to employ this valuable talent. Perhaps all instruction necessary for this may be reduced to three plain rules.

Gain all you can!

Gain all you can. Here we may meet "children of the world" on their own ground. We ought not to gain money at the expense of life or health. Neither should we begin or continue in any business which deprives us of proper seasons for food and sleep in such proportion as our nature requires.

We are to gain all we can without hurting our mind, any more than our body. Therefore we may not engage or continue in any sinful trade; any that is contrary to the law of God or of our country. We are to gain all we can without hurting our neighbor. If we love our neighbor as ourselves, we shall not hurt him or his substance. We cannot, consistent with "brotherly love," sell our goods below the market price. Neither may we gain by hurting our neighbor in his body. Therefore we may not sell what tends to impair health, such as spirituous liquors.

Gain all you can by common sense, by using in your business all the understanding God has given you. Whatever they do who know not God, it is a shame for a Christian not to improve upon them in whatever he takes in hand. Be continually learning—from the experience of others, from your own experience, reading, and reflection—to do better today than yesterday. Make the best of all in your hands.

Save All You Can!

Having gained all you can, by honest wisdom and unwearied diligence, the second rule of Christian prudence is to *save* all you can. Do not throw away your money in idle expenses; expend no part merely to gratify the desire of the flesh, the eye, or the pride of life. Do not waste any part of so precious a talent in superfluous furniture, expensive apparel, or needless ornaments. "What is that to thee?" says our Lord; "follow thou me."

Lay out nothing to gratify "the pride of life," to gain admiration or praise of men. Be content with honor that comes from God. And why throw away money in delicate food, costly apparel, in superfluities of any kind upon your children? Why purchase for them pride, vanity, and foolish, hurtful desires, any more than for yourself? Why be at expense to increase their temptations and snares? Do not leave it to them to throw away if you have reason to believe they would waste what is now in your possession, and "pierce themselves through with many sorrows." Have pity on them.

Give All You Can!

Having first, gained all you can; and secondly, saved all you can; then, thirdly *give* all you can!

To see the ground and reason of this, consider that, when the possessor of heaven and earth brought you into being, he placed you in this world, not as proprietor but as a steward. As such, he entrusted you with goods of various kinds; but the sole property of these can never be alienated from him. As you yourself are not your own but his, such is likewise all that you enjoy, your substance in particular.

He has told you how you are to employ it for him, that all may be acceptable through Jesus Christ; and this easy service he has promised to reward.

Should a doubt arise in your mind concerning what you are going to expend, you have an easy way to remove it. Calmly, seriously enquire:

1. Am I acting therein, not as a proprietor but as steward of my Lord's goods?

2. Am I doing this in obedience to his Word? In what Scripture does he require me so to do?

3. Can I offer this action, this expense, as a sacrifice to God through Jesus Christ?

4. Have I reason to believe that for this I shall have a reward at the resurrection of the just?

You will seldom need more to remove doubt on this matter; but by this fourfold consideration you will receive clear light.

—Abridged from a tract

Appendix B

Regarding Eternal Friendships
as told by Harold Wildish

(Some years ago this beloved Bible teacher recounted the following story at one of our missionary conferences. It first appeared in *The Prairie Overcomer* for September, 1958.)

In British Guiana, where I used to labor some years ago, we had a very fine committee for the British and Foreign Bible Society. We used to meet every three months to plan for the future. On that committee there was an elderly lady—I believe she came from a titled family—who was a very devout Christian. One day she told us this story:

When my father reached his eightieth birthday, we as a family wanted to give him a birthday present. We decided we would give him one from the whole family, rather than many individual gifts. So we gathered a nice sum of money to buy him a present—about £800 (that is, about $2,400). Then came the question: What could we buy him? It's the hardest thing to know what to buy a man of eighty for his birthday.

Finally, the lady told us, they decided that they would ask him what he would like. The old gentleman looked into their faces and said: "Do you mean that you have collected a sum of money to buy me an eightieth birthday present? And you are going to leave it to me to choose what you should get?"

The family answered, "Yes."

"Well," said the old man, "I'll tell you what I would like. I would like my eightieth birthday present to be used to send an edition of the Scriptures in a new language to a tribe of people who have never had the gospel in their own language."

"Do you really mean that?" asked the family.

Well, they went to the British and Foreign Bible Society and put their need before the Society. The manager of the Society responded: "It

148

is an amazing thing. For years missionaries in the Belgian Congo have been working on a certain dialect, and they have actually produced the full manuscript from Genesis to Revelation. We have that manuscript in the Bible House, waiting for the first edition to go out."

The family asked, "How much will it cost?" "About £1,000."

The family passed the hat around again, made up the extra money, and paid for the edition.

About eighteen months afterward, some big packing cases are being put on board ship in London. Now they are going down the coast of Africa. They are being taken from the ship to a river boat, and then from the river boat to a truck. Now they have reached the end of the road and are being broken into bundles for the carriers to carry through the long grass and forest.

At last they reach their destination—the first edition of the Bible in a new language is opened up. And men and women in Africa are receiving the Word of God for the first time to read it in their own language. There are responses for Jesus—"I will trust thee with my soul." "Thank you for dying for me." There are souls being born again through his Word.

Meeting Friends in Glory

Now in imagination can you see the old Englishman when he has gone to glory and is changed into the likeness of Christ, in the great unfoldings of the future. As he meets with the great family circle, he asks one, "I say, where were you saved down in that old world of sin?"

"I was saved in the Congo, the heart of Africa. Where were you saved?"

"Oh, I was saved in old England, you know. I gave my heart to Jesus Christ there."

They are comparing notes. "Let's see. What language did you speak down there?"

A dialect is mentioned.

"Oh, my! My eightieth birthday present went out in the Scriptures in that language. Do you mean to say you were saved by the reading of the Word of God there? Oh, isn't it wonderful!"

And I think they will greet each other with a holy kiss on those hills of glory. He is meeting a friend, an eternal friend, that he has made because of his stewardship. Instead of wasting his goods, he said, in sacrificial devotion, "Take my life and let it be consecrated, Lord, to thee. Take my silver and my gold." Laying his resources in stewardship at the feet of Jesus, he was making friends for eternity.

Appendix C

In the Service of the King

A missionary couple in Bangkok, Thailand, writes:

One of the compensations of our work in Bangkok is that we are kept in close touch with worldwide missions, for we frequently entertain missionaries passing through Bangkok on their way home for furlough or coming back to the field.

Among these recently were two Japanese young men on their way from Japan to Laos, where they are to be missionaries among the tribespeople. They have had wide experience as evangelists in their own country, but their churches were given a missionary vision and looked out beyond their own needy land to the unreached tribes in isolated areas of Laos. In true New Testament style their Japanese church set apart these two young workers and sent them forth as foreign missionaries to Laos.

The young men gave their testimonies at one of our two weekly prayer meetings.

The aged father of one of these missionaries had stood on the wharf in Japan among a great crowd of Christians who had gathered there to bid the young men farewell. An American missionary came to sympathize with the father and said, "Honorable sir, you must feel this parting very keenly, but be of good cheer—you will see your son again when he returns to Japan for furlough."

The old father replied, "Pastor, when we Japanese people sent our sons to the war and saw them go overseas to fight for their country, we did not expect to see them again. In fact we told them, 'Do not return again—give your life for your country.' Now I am sending this young son of mine across the seas to another and more glorious conflict—to the service of the King of kings. Should I hope to see him again on the shores of Japan? No; we give him gladly to service in Laos, and we do not expect to see him again on this earth."

—*The Millions*

Appendix D

A Strange but True Story
by Mrs. H. Grattan Guinness

A wealthy farmer who cultivated some thousands of acres had by his benevolence endeared himself greatly to his large staff of laborers. He had occasion to leave the country in which his property was situated, for some years.

But before doing so, he gave his people clearly to understand that he wished the whole of the cultivated land to be kept in hand, and all the unreclaimed moor and marsh lands to be enclosed and drained and brought into cultivation; that even the hills were to be terraced, and the poor mountain pastures manured, so that no single corner of the estate should remain neglected and barren. Ample resources were left for the execution of these works, and there were sufficient hands to have accomplished the whole within the first few years of the proprietor's absence.

He was detained in the country to which he had been called very many years. Those whom he had left as children were men and women when he came back, so the number of his tenantry and laborers was vastly multiplied. Was the task he had given them to do accomplished?

Alas! No. Bog and moor and mountain waste were only wilder and more desolate than ever. Fine rich virgin soil by thousands of acres was bearing only briars and thistles. Meadow after meadow was utterly barren for want of culture. Nay, by far the greater part of the farm seemed never to have been visited by his servants.

Had they been idle? Some had. But large numbers had been industrious enough. They had expended a vast amount of labor, and skilled labor, too, but they had bestowed it all on the park immediately around the house. This had been cultivated to such a pitch of perfection that the workmen had scores of times quarreled with one another because the operations of each workman had interfered with those of his neighbor.

And a vast amount of labor had been lost in sowing the very same patch, for instance, with corn fifty times over in one season, so that the seed never had time to germinate and grow and bear fruit; in caring for the forest trees, as if they had been tender saplings; in manuring the soils already too fat, and watering pastures already too wet.

The farmer was positively astonished at the misplaced ingenuity with which labor and seed and manure, skill and time and strength, had been wasted with no result. The very same amount of toil and capital, *expended according to his directions,* would have brought the whole demesne (estate) into culture, and yielded a noble revenue. But season after season rolled away in sad succession, leaving those unbounded acres of various but all *reclaimable* soils, barren and useless; and as to the park, it would have been far more productive and perfect had it been relieved of the extraordinary and unaccountable amount of energy expended on it.

Why did these laborers act so absurdly? Did they wish to labor in vain? On the contrary! They were forever craving for fruit, coveting good crops, longing for great results. Did they not wish to carry out the farmer's views about his property? Well, they seemed to have that desire, for they were always reading the directions he wrote, and said continually to one another, "You know, we have to bring the *whole property* into order." But they did not do it.

Some few tried and ploughed up a little plot here and there, and sowed corn and other crops. Perhaps these failed, and so the rest got discouraged? Oh, no; they saw that the yield was magnificent; far richer in proportion than they got themselves.

They clearly perceived that, but yet they failed to follow this good example. Nay—when the labor of a few in some distant valley had resulted in a crop they were all unable to gather by themselves, the others would not even go and help them to bring home the sheaves! *They preferred watching for weeds among the roses, in the overcrowded garden, and counting the blades of grass in the park and the leaves on the trees.*

Then they were fools, surely, not wise men? Traitors, not true servants to their lord? Ah, I can't tell! You must ask him that! I only know their master said, "Go ye into all the world and preach the gospel to every creature," and that 1900 years afterward they had *not even mentioned that there was a gospel to one half of the world.*

"And why call ye me Lord, Lord, and DO NOT THE THINGS I SAY?"

Appendix E

A World "Without"

A great missionary of the past generation wrote:

A great "without" is written over heathenism. Men and women are *without* a Bible, *without* a Sunday, and *without* righteousness. They have homes *without* peace, marriage *without* sanctity. Their young men and women are *without* ideals, the little children *without* purity, the mothers *without* wisdom or self-control. There is poverty *without* relief, sickness *without* skill or care, sorrow *without* sympathy, sin *without* remedy, death *without* hope *without* Christ.

All this is wrapped up in the words, "*without* Christ." This is why Christ has told us to go "into all the world, and preach the gospel." This is why we urge you to give and pray *without* stint, for the only answer to the world *without is* to have Christ *WITHIN*.

Without the Book

In the year 1831 four Nez Perce chiefs made their way over the Rockies and were found on the street in St. Louis, asking, "Where is the white man's Book of heaven?" General Clark befriended them and showed them everything of interest in the town. Two of the four fell ill and died. Before the remaining Indians departed, General Clark gave a feast to them and in a farewell address at this feast one of the two poured forth his burden of sorrow in words of pathetic eloquence as follows:

I came to you over the trail of many moons from the setting sun. You were friends of my fathers, who have all gone the long way. I came with an eye partly open for my people who sit in darkness. I go back to them with both eyes closed. How can I go back blind to my blinded people? I made my way to you with strong arms through many enemies and strange lands that I might carry back much to them. I go back with both arms broken and empty!

155

Two fathers came with us; they were braves of many snows and wars. We leave them asleep here by your great water and teepees. They were tired in many moons, and their moccasins wore out. My people sent me to get the white man's Book of heaven. You took me to where you allow your women to dance, as we do not ours, and the Book was not there! You showed me images of the Great Spirit and pictures of the good land beyond, but the Book was not among them to tell me the way.

I am going back the long trail to my people in the dark land. You make my feet heavy with gifts and my moccasins will grow old carrying them, and yet the Book is not among them! When I tell my poor, blind people after one more snow, in the big council, that I did not bring the Book, no word will be spoken by our old men or by our young braves. One by one they will rise up and go out in silence. My people will die in darkness, and they will go on a long path to other hunting grounds. No white man will go with them and no white man's Book to make the way plain. I have no more words.

Also from Kingsley Press:

AN ORDERED LIFE

AN AUTOBIOGRAPHY BY G. H. LANG

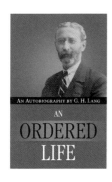

G. H. Lang was a remarkable Bible teacher, preacher and writer of a past generation who should not be forgotten by today's Christians. He inherited the spiritual "mantle" of such giants in the faith as George Müller, Anthony Norris Groves and other notable saints among the early Brethren movement. He traveled all over the world with no fixed means of support other than prayer and faith and no church or other organization to depend on. Like Mr. Müller before him, he told his needs to no one but God. Many times his faith was tried to the limit, as funds for the next part of his journey arrived only at the last minute and from unexpected sources.

This autobiography traces in precise detail the dealings of God with his soul, from the day of his conversion at the tender age of seven, through the twilight years when bodily infirmity restricted most of his former activities. You will be amazed, as you read these pages, to see how quickly and continually a soul can grow in grace and in the knowledge of spiritual things if they will wholly follow the Lord.

Horace Bushnell once wrote that every man's life is a plan of God, and that it's our duty as human beings to find and follow that plan. As Mr. Lang looks back over his long and varied life in the pages of this book, he frequently points out the many times God prepared him in the present for some future work or role. Spiritual life applications abound throughout the book, making it not just a life story but a spiritual training manual of sorts. Preachers will find sermon starters and illustrations in every chapter. Readers of all kinds will benefit from this close-up view of the dealings of God with the soul of one who made it his life's business to follow the Lamb wherever He should lead.

Buy online at our website: **www.KingsleyPress.com**
Also available as an eBook for Kindle, Nook and iBooks.

The Revival We Need

by Oswald J. Smith

When Oswald J. Smith wrote this book almost a hundred years ago he felt the most pressing need of the worldwide church was true revival—the kind birthed in desperate prayer and accompanied by deep conviction for sin, godly sorrow, and deep repentance, resulting in a living, victorious faith. If he were alive today he would surely conclude that the need has only become more acute with the passing years.

The author relates how there came a time in his own ministry when he became painfully aware that his efforts were not producing spiritual results. His intense study of the New Testament and past revivals only deepened this conviction. The Word of God, which had proved to be a hammer, a fire and a sword in the hands of apostles and revivalists of bygone days, was powerless in his hands. But as he prayed and sought God in dead earnest for the outpouring of the Holy Spirit, things began to change. Souls came under conviction, repented of their sins, and were lastingly changed.

The earlier chapters of the book contain Smith's heart-stirring messages on the need for authentic revival: how to prepare the way for the Spirit's moving, the tell-tale signs that the work is genuine, and the obstacles that can block up the channels of blessing. These chapters are laced with powerful quotations from revivalists and soul-winners of former times, such as David Brainerd, William Bramwell, John Wesley, Charles Finney, Evan Roberts and many others. The latter chapters detail Smith's own quest for the enduement of power, his soul-travail, and the spiritual fruit that followed.

In his foreword to this book, Jonathan Goforth writes, "Mr. Smith's book, *The Revival We Need*, for its size is the most powerful plea for revival I have ever read. He has truly been led by the Spirit of God in preparing it. To his emphasis for the need of a Holy Spirit revival I can give the heartiest amen. What I saw of revival in Korea and in China is in fullest accord with the revival called for in this book."

Buy online at our website: **www.KingsleyPress.com**
Also available as an eBook for Kindle, Nook and iBooks.

Lord, Teach Us to Pray
By Alexander Whyte

Dr. Alexander Whyte (1836-1921) was widely acknowledged to be the greatest Scottish preacher of his day. He was a mighty pulpit orator who thundered against sin, awakening the consciences of his hearers, and then gently leading them to the Savior. He was also a great teacher, who would teach a class of around 500 young men after Sunday night service, instructing them in the way of the Lord more perfectly.

In the later part of Dr. Whyte's ministry, one of his pet topics was prayer. Luke 11:1 was a favorite text and was often used in conjunction with another text as the basis for his sermons on this subject. The sermons printed here represent only a few of the many delivered. But each one is deeply instructive, powerful and convicting.

Nobody else could have preached these sermons; after much reading and re-reading of them that remains the most vivid impression. There can be few more strongly personal documents in the whole literature of the pulpit. . . . When all is said, there is something here that defies analysis—something titanic, something colossal, which makes ordinary preaching seem to lie a long way below such heights as gave the vision in these words, such forces as shaped their appeal. We are driven back on the mystery of a great soul, dealt with in God's secret ways and given more than the ordinary measure of endowment and grace. His hearers have often wondered at his sustained intensity; as Dr. Joseph Parker once wrote of him: "many would have announced the chaining of Satan for a thousand years with less expenditure of vital force" than Dr. Whyte gave to the mere announcing of a hymn. —*From the Preface*

Buy online at our website: **www.KingsleyPress.com**
Also available as an eBook for Kindle, Nook and iBooks.

The Way of the Cross
by J. Gregory Mantle

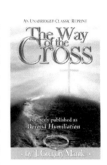

"**D**YING to self is the *one only way* to life in God," writes Dr. Mantle in this classic work on the cross. "The end of self is the one condition of the promised blessing, and he that is not willing to die to things sinful, *yea, and to things lawful,* if they come between the spirit and God, cannot enter that world of light and joy and peace, provided on this side of heaven's gates, where thoughts and wishes, words and works, delivered from the perverting power of self—revolve round Jesus Christ, as the planets revolve around the central sun. . . .

"It is a law of dynamics that two objects cannot occupy the same space at the same time, and if we are ignorant of the crucifixion of the self-life as an experimental experience, we cannot be filled with the Holy Spirit. 'If thy heart,' says Arndt in his *True Christianity,* 'be full of the world, there will be no room for the Spirit of God to enter; for where the one is the other cannot be.' If, on the contrary, we have endorsed our Saviour's work as the destroyer of the works of the devil, and have claimed to the full the benefits of His death and risen life, what hinders the complete and abiding possession of our being by the Holy Spirit but our unbelief?"

Rev. J. Gregory Mantle (1853 - 1925) had a wide and varied ministry in Great Britain, America, and around the world. For many years he was the well-loved Superintendent of the flourishing Central Hall in Deptford, England, as well as a popular speaker at Keswick and other large conventions for the deepening of spiritual life. He spent the last twelve years of his life in America, where he was associated with Dr. A. B. Simpson and the Christian and Missionary Alliance. He traveled extensively, holding missions and conventions all over the States. He was an avid supporter of foreign missions throughout his entire career. He also edited a missionary paper, and wrote several books.

GIPSY SMITH
HIS LIFE AND WORK

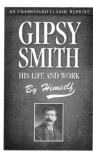

This autobiography of Gipsy Smith (1860-1947) tells the fascinating story of how God's amazing grace reached down into the life of a poor, uneducated gipsy boy and sent him singing and preaching all over Britain and America until he became a household name in many parts and influenced the lives of millions for Christ. He was born and raised in a gipsy tent to parents who made a living selling baskets, tinware and clothes pegs. His father was in and out of jail for various offences, but was gloriously converted during an evangelistic meeting. His mother died when he was only five years old.

Converted at the age of sixteen, Gipsy taught himself to read and write and began to practice preaching. His beautiful singing voice earned him the nickname "the singing gipsy boy," as he sang hymns to the people he met. At age seventeen he became an evangelist with the Christian Mission (which became the Salvation Army) and began to attract large crowds. Leaving the Salvation Army in 1882, he became an itinerant evangelist working with a variety of organizations. It is said that he never had a meeting without conversions. He was a born orator. One of the Boston papers described him as "the greatest of his kind on earth, a spiritual phenomenon, an intellectual prodigy and a musical and oratorical paragon."

His autobiography is full of anedotes and stories from his preaching experiences in many different places. It's a book you won't want to put down until you're finished!

THE AWAKENING

By Marie Monsen

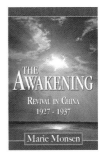

REVIVAL! It was a long time coming. For twenty long years Marie Monsen prayed for revival in China. She had heard reports of how God's Spirit was being poured out in abundance in other countries, particularly in nearby Korea; so she began praying for funds to be able to travel there in order to bring back some of the glowing coals to her own mission field. But that was not God's way. The still, small voice of God seemed to whisper, "What is happening in Korea can happen in China if you will pay the price in prayer." Marie Monsen took up the challenge and gave her solemn promise: "Then I will pray until I receive."

The Awakening is Miss Monsen's own vivid account of the revival that came in answer to prayer. Leslie Lyall calls her the "pioneer" of the revival movement—the handmaiden upon whom the Spirit was first poured out. He writes: "Her surgical skill in exposing the sins hidden within the Church and lurking behind the smiling exterior of many a trusted Christian—even many a trusted Christian leader—and her quiet insistence on a clear-cut experience of the new birth set the pattern for others to follow."

The emphasis in these pages is on the place given to prayer both before and during the revival, as well as on the necessity of self-emptying, confession, and repentance in order to make way for the infilling of the Spirit.

One of the best ways to stir ourselves up to pray for revival in our own generation is to read the accounts of past awakenings, such as those found in the pages of this book. Surely God is looking for those in every generation who will solemnly take up the challenge and say, with Marie Monsen, "I will pray until I receive."

Buy online at our website: **www.KingsleyPress.com**
Also available as an eBook for Kindle, Nook and iBooks.

A Present Help
By Marie Monsen

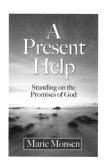

Does your faith in the God of the impossible need reviving? Do you think that stories of walls of fire and hosts of guardian angels protecting God's children are only for Bible times? Then you should read the amazing accounts in this book of how God and His unseen armies protected and guided Marie Monsen, a Norwegian missionary to China, as she traveled through bandit-ridden territory spreading the Gospel of Jesus Christ and standing on the promises of God. You will be amazed as she tells of an invading army of looters who ravaged a whole city, yet were not allowed to come near her mission compound because of angels standing sentry over it. Your heart will thrill as she tells of being held captive on a ship for twenty-three days by pirates whom God did not allow to harm her, but instead were compelled to listen to her message of a loving Savior who died for their sin. As you read the many stories in this small volume your faith will be strengthened by the realization that our God is a living God who can still bring protection and peace in the midst of the storms of distress, confusion and terror—a very present help in trouble.

Buy online at our website: **www.KingsleyPress.com**
Also available as an eBook for Kindle, Nook and iBooks.

ANTHONY NORRIS GROVES
SAINT AND PIONEER
by G. H. Lang

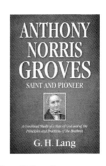

Although his name is little known in Christian cirlces today, Anthony Norris Groves (1795-1853) was, according to the writer of this book, one of the most influential men of the nineteenth century. He was what might be termed a spiritual pioneer, forging a path through unfamiliar territory in order that others might follow. One of those who followed him was George Müller, known to the world as one who in his lifetime cared for over ten thousand orphans without any appeal for human aid, instead trusting God alone to provide for the daily needs of this large enterprise.

In 1825 Groves wrote a booklet called *Christian Devotedness* in which he encouraged fellow believers and especially Christian workers to take literally Jesus' command not to lay up treasures on earth, but rather to give away their savings and possessions toward the spread of the gospel and to embark on a life of faith in God alone for the necessaries of life. Groves himself took this step of faith: he gave away his fortune, left his lucrative dental practice in England, and went to Baghdad to establish the first Protestant mission to Arabic-speaking Muslims. His going was not in connection with any church denomination or missionary society, as he sought to rely on God alone for needed finances. He later went to India also.

His approach to missions was to simplify the task of churches and missions by returning to the methods of Christ and His apostles, and to help indigenous converts form their own churches without dependence on foreign support. His ideas were considered radical at the time but later became widely accepted in evangelical circles.

Groves was a leading figure in the early days of what Robert Govett would later call the mightiest movement of the Spirit of God since Pentecost—a movement that became known simply as the Brethren. In this book G. H. Lang combines a study of the life and influence of Anthony Norris Groves with a survey of the original principles and practices of the Brethren movement.

MEMOIRS OF DAVID STONER

EDITED BY
WILLIAM DAWSON & JOHN HANNAH

The name of David Stoner (1794-1826) deserves to be ranked alongside those of Robert Murray McCheyne, David Brainerd and Henry Martyn. Like them, he died at a relatively young age; and like them, his life was marked by a profound hunger and thirst for God and intense passion for souls. Stoner was saved at twelve years of age and from that point until his untimely death twenty years later his soul was continually on full stretch for God.

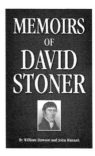

This book tells the story of his short but amazing life: his godly up-gringing, his radical conversion, his call to preach, his amazing success as a Wesleyan Methodist preacher, his patience in tribulation and sickness, and his glorious departure to be with Christ forever. Many pages are devoted to extracts from his personal diary which give an amazing glimpse into the heart of one whose desires were all aflame for more of God.

Oswald J. Smith, in his soul-stirring book, *The Revival We Need,* wrote the following: "Have been reading the diary of David Stoner. How I thank God for it! He is another Brainerd. Have been much helped, but how ashamed and humble I feel as I read it! Oh, how he thirsted and searched after God! How he agonized and travailed! And he died at 32."

You, too can be much helped in your spiritual life as you study the life of this youthful saint of a past generation.

"Be instant and constant in prayer. Study, books, eloquence, fine sermons are all nothing without prayer. Prayer brings the Spirit, the life, the power." —*David Stoner*

Buy online at our website: **www.KingsleyPress.com**
Also available as an eBook for Kindle, Nook and iBooks.

The Christian Hero
A Sketch of the Life of Robert Annan

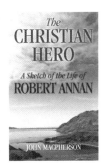

If you've never heard of Robert Annan of Dundee, otherwise known as "the Christian Hero," prepare to be astounded at the amazing grace of God in his life as you turn the pages of this incredible little biography. Its thrilling story will stir you to the depths and almost certainly drive you to your knees with an increased desire to be used for God's glory.

The record of his beginning years reads much like that of John Newton—a life of wandering far from God in the ways of sin and rebellion. At least once he miraculously escaped death through the overruling providence of God. As time passed, he became thoroughly discontented with his sinful life; but he didn't want anything to do with God or Christianity. He thought he could overcome sin and live a morally good life by his own efforts. He soon discovered, however, that he was no match for sin or Satan; and casting himself entirely on God's grace and mercy in Jesus Christ, he was gloriously saved.

From the very first day of his conversion, he became a tireless seeker of lost souls. He worked during the day time as a stone mason, but his evenings and weekends were spent preaching in the streets or in homes. Frequently he would spend whole nights in secret prayer, pleading at the throne of grace for lost sinners. As he went to his employment in the early mornings, he would often write Scripture verses on the pavement for others to read as they passed by on their way to work or school. Thus he was instant in season and out of season, using every opportunity to present to men the claims of Jesus Christ and the reality of heaven, hell, and the judgment that awaits every human soul.

Read his story and be amazed, remembering that what God did for Robert Annan he can and will do for anyone.

Buy online at our website: **www.KingsleyPress.com**
Also available as an eBook for Kindle, Nook and iBooks.